What's the
Best That Could
Happen?

DEBBIE MILLER

What's the BEST That Could Happen?

New Possibilities for Teachers & Readers

Heinemann
Portsmouth, NH

Heinemann

361 Hanover Street

Portsmouth, NH 03801–3912

www.heinemann.com

Offices and agents throughout the world

The author and publisher wish to thank those who have generously given permission to reprint borrowed material:

Excerpts from *Choice Words: How Our Language Affects Children's Learning* by Peter Johnston. Copyright © 2003. Reproduced with permission of Stenhouse Publishers. www.stenhouse.com.

Library of Congress Cataloging-in-Publication Data

Name: Miller, Debbie, author.

Title: What's the best that could happen? : new possibilities for teachers & readers / Debbie Miller.

Description: Portsmouth, NH : Heinemann, [2018] | Includes bibliographical references.

Identifiers: LCCN 2018023827 | ISBN 9780325093116

Subjects: LCSH: Questioning. | Reading.

Classification: LCC LB1027.44 .M55 2018 | DDC 371.3/7—dc23

LC record available at https://lccn.loc.gov/2018023827

Acquisitions Editor: Margaret LaRaia

Production Editor: Sean Moreau

Cover and Interior Designer: Suzanne Heiser

Interior Photographer: Sherry Day

Cover Image: Gordon Saunders / Getty Images

Interior Image: olegagafonov / Getty Images

Typesetter: Suzanne Heiser

Manufacturing: Steve Bernier

Printed in the United States of America on acid-free paper

22 21 20 19 18 VP 1 2 3 4 5

For Eliot, Finley, Frankie, Cora,

and children everywhere—

may your brilliance, goodness, and

light shine forever bright.

CONTENTS

ACKNOWLEDGMENTS

With gratitude and love to everyone who has helped me make this book . . .

Emiliano, and all the children I've been lucky to work with all these years, you've taught me so much! I've been sharing your stories with teachers everywhere—thank you for trusting me, believing in yourself, and inspiring so many others.

Sam Bennett, thank you for making me smarter, occasionally making my head explode (in a good way!), and always having my back. You, my friend, are making a difference, one district at a time. XO

Anne Goudvis, Stephanie Harvey, Ellin Keene, Cris Tovani, and Kristin Venable, you are somehow always with me. (Long live the PEBC!)

Emily Callahan, you are an inspiration to so many teachers and children, especially me! Your boundless energy, love of children, and unwavering belief in what they can do are hallmarks of your work. Being with you in your classroom always makes me wistful for my own.

Karen Cangelose, I just can't read Mo Willems without thinking of you! Thank you for years of collaboration, learning, and laughter and all those after-school dinners with Emily at Trezo Mare. I can't wait to learn what you decide to do next.

Barb Smith, your passion for teaching and learning is contagious! Thank you for your friendship and conversation about the things that matter most. (And I'm so happy Eliot and Frankie get to have you for their teacher!)

Amy Brock, Megan Burns, Emily Finney, and Susan Phillips, I'll never forget the day you decided to "let it go." It was pure joy watching you and your children own the learning. You really did (and do) make the world a better place.

Jacklyn Brunk, I'll always remember the two days I spent with you, your kids, and all those books by Chris Van Allsburg. We know that teaching isn't about perfection, but on that first day together, I wouldn't have changed a thing—it was a "heart-hitting" day. Thank you for jumping in with me!

Jenn Phillips, we always say we're better together, and it's true! I've loved working and learning alongside you, and most of all that we've become fast friends. Thank you for your unwavering belief in coaches, teachers, and children in Blue Springs and beyond. (Not to mention all those Starbucks runs and pickups and deliveries to and from the Hilton Garden Inn!)

Annette Seago, you are a force of nature. Thank you for your tireless and steadfast support of coaches, teachers, children, and the community of Blue Springs. And me.

Casi Hodge, Lisa Friesen, and Chad Sutton in North Kansas City, I've loved working and learning with you. Chad—your vision for kids is becoming reality! (Nice work, everyone!)

Lindsay Yates, Emily Callahan, and Nicole Johnson, thank you for letting us spend time with you and take photos of your beautiful classroom, school, and children. Crossroads Academy–Quality Hill is an amazing place for teachers and children to teach, learn, and thrive.

Steve Bernier, Sherry Day, Dennis Doyle, Josh Evans, Lisa Fowler, Suzanne Heiser, Sean Moreau, Jane Orr, Edie Davis Quinn, Beth Tripp, and Brett Whitmarsh at Heinemann, I'm in awe of you! I so appreciate your time, attention to detail, and expertise on my behalf—you truly are a dream team.

And . . .

Margaret LaRaia, this book wouldn't be in the world without you! I came with an idea, and you helped me shape it into something beautiful and real. I loved all our figuring-things-out conversations—I miss them, and you, already! Thank you for your honest feedback, for believing in this project and me, and for advocating for children and teachers everywhere and always.

And because I always save the best for last . . .

Thank you, babe, for the walks, and talks, and big love. Your encouragement and support were all I needed to keep going. (Now it's your turn for a project!) And while I'm at it, thank you for believing in me, and us, and sharing your life and love for forty-seven years and counting. (What?) And to Noah, Chad, Courtney, Rachel, and our four delightful granddaughters, you enrich our lives beyond measure. We love, love, love you!

We Can Do This

Asking Beautiful Questions

Impressed by the innovations around him, journalist Warren Berger decided to investigate how designers, inventors, and engineers came up with ideas to solve problems. In his inquiry into how the world's leading innovators and creative minds approached challenges, he found no fixed answer for their success.

But in searching for common denominators among these brilliant change makers, he kept finding that many of them were exceptionally good at asking questions (which led him to write his 2014 book *A More Beautiful Question*). For some of them, their greatest successes—their breakthrough inventions and solutions they'd found to tricky problems—could be traced to a question (or a series of questions) they'd formulated and then answered,

Berger laments the fact that for too many of us, our impulse is to keep plowing ahead, doing what we've always done, and rarely stepping back to question whether we're on the right path. On the big questions of finding meaning, fulfillment, and happiness, he says we're deluged with answers—in the form of off-the-shelf advice, tips, and strategies from experts and gurus. It shouldn't be any wonder if those generic solutions don't quite fit: to get to our answers, we must formulate and work through the questions ourselves.

I think the same might be true for teachers. So many different voices—principals, coaches, programs, policies, standards—pepper us with answers that don't quite fit. And do we even know what the questions are or who is asking them?

Sometimes we are the ones pushing ahead as if on autopilot, with no time to step back and question and reflect on what we're doing, where we're going, what we believe, and who we are. It's as if our days are more about *getting* through than *thinking* through, checking off the boxes instead of being present, delighting in children, and working hard to meet individual needs in authentic ways.

But what if we worked together to change all that? What if we joined the ranks of the change makers and committed the time and effort it would take to formulate and work through our own beautiful questions? Could these actions change the narrative about how schools work? Could teachers be the ones to begin real conversations with each other and those in power?

Yes! And if we do, I'm betting we'll have inspiring and influential stories to tell about who we are, what we can do, and most especially what children can do when we put them in the forefront of our minds. And hearts.

Berger defines a beautiful question this way: "an ambitious yet actionable question that can begin to shift the way we perceive or think about something, and might serve as a catalyst to bring about change" (2014, 8). He asks us to think about this: "Why are we doing this particular thing in this particular way?"

Paying Attention to What Doesn't Feel Right

When I do demonstration teaching in schools across the country, teachers sometimes worry:

- ❖ "But I can't do it that way. When I teach my minilessons, I have to follow these four steps. In order."

- ❖ "I need to follow the rules for workshop. I don't think what you're showing us is allowed."

- ❖ "I've been told I have to teach content this way, so I can't really do that."

Of course it would be a different story if they weren't interested in and intrigued about what they'd seen and heard, if they didn't believe it would help children become better readers. But they say they can't after they say they wish they could. Why do so many of us feel like we can't try new things or do things differently from how we've been told? And what must that feel like when walking into school each day?

Testing, mandates, reading series adoptions—all these add to the intense pressure we can feel. Compliance at least puts us in charge of something, especially when we're under pressure and feel in charge of little else. But what does that mean for children's learning, I wonder? Does being under pressure—and feeling restricted—cause us to put children under pressure and restrict them too?

We've all had times in our lives when we've been stuck: we've gone through the motions of teaching without being present in our bodies, hearts, and minds.

When this happens, the good emotions feel a little further away and the bad ones a little closer. And then, hopefully, something snaps us out of it: we get inspired, or we get fed up enough to change. That all begins with paying attention when things don't feel right. Noticing when we feel like we don't have a choice or voice can allow us to recognize where and how we do. And it can start by reframing what we think of as a "given" as a question instead:

- ❖ Does the minilesson really have to follow these four steps?
- ❖ Are there rules to workshop?
- ❖ Does teaching this content mean I can't do that?

Simply asking the question gives us some of our power back, and pursuing the answer makes us more powerful still. When we examine our goals, we'll soon find that each of these questions can be answered with "No"—we can say no to the too-rigid, limiting expectations for our teaching and we can say yes to questions that invite us to reflect, create, and be present as the creative, brilliant educators we can be.

- ❖ If the minilesson doesn't have to follow four steps, what might I do to better serve children's learning?
- ❖ If there are fewer rules to workshop than I thought, how might I make my workshop more focused on the children in my classroom and less on the rules?
- ❖ How can I fulfill my obligation to teach this content in a way that engages and expands what's possible for children?

Notice that these questions focus on children and our behaviors rather than on strict definitions of established teaching structures. No structure, no standard, no unit, no expectation matters until we take it off the paper and bring it to life for children and ourselves. Teaching is about taking responsibility, not about following orders. Teaching is about creativity, not about limiting possibilities because we have to stick to someone else's script. Teaching is about relationships with children, not about rigid structures.

Asking, "What If?": Creating Space for Possibility

Literacy researcher Anne Haas Dyson reminds us what children need from us: "A child must have some version of, 'Yes, I imagine I can do this.' And the teacher must view the present child as capable, and on that basis, imagine new possibilities" (1993, 396–397).

For a child to imagine he can do something, he needs time to explore, discover, and reflect on who he is as a learner, what he needs, and why. And he needs someone with a broader sense of the present moment, someone who understands that what he is doing is significant because it is part of the bigger picture.

Most children can't do this without us.

That's why teachers must also have some version of "Yes, I imagine we can do this." Before we can support and encourage children to find their way, we have to believe that we're up to finding our way, too. Before we can trust children to make decisions about what they need and when they need it, we need to know how it feels to make decisions that matter to us and the children we teach. And before we can imagine new possibilities for children, we have to imagine new possibilities for ourselves.

We have to learn to be comfortable being uncomfortable.

Sometimes it's the small things that can liberate us and instill the early sparks of agency, ownership, and independence. Even something as mundane as how we use sticky notes helps us be clear about what our mandates or restrictions actually are. Can we begin to change the narrative from lamenting what we can't and don't do to imagining all the extraordinary things teachers, and the children they teach, can and will do?

That's my goal. No teacher wants to be a fake teacher. And no child delights in learning from a script. Teachers dream of being real teachers—teachers who read, write, think, collaborate, get smarter, and plan for the real children who walk through their doors every day. When teachers are trusted, valued, and supported, children are, too. All of us—teachers and children alike—hunger to figure things out, forge new paths, create, question, and learn.

We all have difficult moments in our teaching, and without a question to drive us forward, we can get stuck. But that difficult moment might *be* the question we need to ask ourselves. Questions can bring a positive attention, creating a presence in the moment. When I ask children, "Are you the kind of kid who . . . ?", I'm inviting them to imagine a new possibility for themselves, one in which they have more power than they did before. I want those new possibilities for teachers, too. Are you the kind of teacher who is ready to try something new, something that will make your students stronger, more joyful readers and bring you greater joy in your work? I think you are.

Every year, I commit to trying something new because it's fun to learn more about something we're unsure about—it motivates us and is part of being a professional. I do it for children, of course, but I also do it for myself. That's what makes us joyful: it's something we do for ourselves *and* for children.

When we do, we're present in our teaching. We're flesh and blood, imperfect human beings who want to grow and learn alongside our children. We're strong enough to set aside judgment and discomfort and choose to focus on how to make things better. Each day we come to school we don't ask only our students, "What did you learn about yourself as a reader today?" We also ask ourselves, "What did

What if I designed my prompts to encourage children to be more independent?

Beautiful Questions About the Teaching of Reading

What If Each Day's Teaching Focused on Children's Agency?

What If We Made What Children Make and Do Our Priority?

What If Our Classroom Environment and Routines Offered Choice?

What If We Owned the Units We Are Asked to Teach?

What If Read-Aloud Sustained Children's Independent Thinking?

Post at RR table w/ my What if... question

I learn about myself as a teacher and my children as readers that I didn't know before? What are my goals for tomorrow based on what I learned today?" These are the essential beautiful questions that drive our teaching and our students' learning forward. To deny that distances us from the joy in our professional lives.

Asking questions leads to opportunities—it's about growth, openness, and a willingness to change, which top-down models don't allow. It's a way for us to focus our thinking and be present in the lives we've chosen to live. Asking the question is the essential behavior of teaching. It's not a perfect call-and-response but a messy business of wondering, stumbling, and figuring things out. It requires bravery and commitment, but that's what teaching is. It's a joyful, creative, purposeful profession. If you feel you've lost even some of your passion for teaching, I would love to help give it back to you. So, in this book, we'll talk about creating beautiful questions about the teaching of reading. To help you take on the process of asking beautiful questions, I'll share how I got to some beautiful questions about teaching reading and what I did with them as I worked with teachers in classrooms across the country.

These five questions shouldn't limit your personal inquiry in any way. The questions aren't final; they're "more beautiful," as Berger (2014) says, always in a stage of revision, like our teaching and children's learning. I hope these questions serve as examples for asking your own beautiful questions about the teaching of reading. Yes, each chapter will share practical insights and deeper understandings that I hope will benefit you and your children, but the larger purpose is to show you the process of asking questions. We (other teachers and I) arrived at these questions because something didn't feel right, or we experienced joy at seeing children do something unexpected, and wanted to understand why and how it happened. Then, we grappled with some messiness: what were we going to do with these questions? We found answers that inspired something new and worthy in our teaching, but even better, we found ourselves changed by asking the questions. I want that for you, too.

This book is about owning our teaching and making decisions based on who we are and what's best for the children in our classroom today. That all sounds ambitious and brave . . . and the work is—teaching is—but it happens in so many small and simple ways. My wish is for you to think about what you do and ask your own beautiful questions, so that you and your children can thrive and view yourselves and each other as valuable, idea-filled, creative, and contributing humans who own your teaching and learning. Be open and receptive to possibilities! Think: "What if we did it this way?"

Teaching for agency sets students up for generative acts, for creativity, for problem solving in the most powerful way.

—PETER H. JOHNSTON
CHOICE WORDS: HOW OUR LANGUAGE AFFECTS CHILDREN'S LEARNING (2003, 31)

Meet Emiliano.

CHAPTER 1

What If Each Day's Teaching Focused on Children's Agency?

▓ Finding Our Way to a Beautiful Question: The Disengaged Child

We've all known a child like Emiliano. He's the one who is in and out of the classroom, needing a drink, the bathroom, the nurse. On this particular day, I find Emiliano inside the classroom, his head on his desk, staring at I'm not sure what. Another child tells me Emiliano's in trouble and I shouldn't talk to him right now; Emiliano affirms this comment by turning his head the other way and staring at something else.

As you might imagine, Emiliano gets lots of attention for all the wrong reasons. His name is on the board day after day, followed by one check mark after another. The intention is to help him, but I wonder, "Could all the attention given to him and his behavior actually *encourage* him to misbehave?"

Everyone wants to be noticed. Even being noticed for the wrong reasons is better than not being noticed at all. So now, at the tender age of nine, Emiliano has taken on the identity of a child who doesn't participate in his learning, an identity no child should call his own. This is how he views himself, and this is how almost everyone else at school views him too.

It's easy to get into the habit of complaining about a child's behavior, lack of effort, negative attitude, or all of these. We drive to school with resolve to be more understanding and kind. But it all falls apart by ten o'clock when a child stomps out of the room, refuses to open her book, or rolls her eyes and groans at a mere suggestion.

No teacher disengages from a child on purpose—we're doing the best we can on any given day. But I wonder if we default to rigid, authoritarian systems when we ourselves feel lost and frustrated and don't know what else to do. And maybe when we focus our attention on behavior and compliance, it's hard to get beyond those feelings and recognize the gifts this child has to give. We get stuck there, in the difficulty. We know things could be otherwise, but we're not quite sure how or where to begin. We're caught between feeling too inadequate to try and understanding we need to do something.

We've all been kept awake because of the inevitable challenges of teaching, but how do we get up and out the next morning and greet the day? We try to look past ourselves, to avoid making assumptions or taking things personally, and to understand the child feels less than, too. We do our best to hold ourselves responsible and resolve to deepen our relationships with the children who test us, the ones who make us feel less than. We realize that, despite difficulty, we have some agency in figuring out a brighter path for these children and ourselves.

What's the Best That Could Happen? Agency Fosters Engagement

We can't permanently isolate ourselves from difficulty and neither can children, so we maintain practices that focus on instilling children's agency throughout the day. We might start with "Why aren't things going right for this child?" but we'll improve the situation only when we take

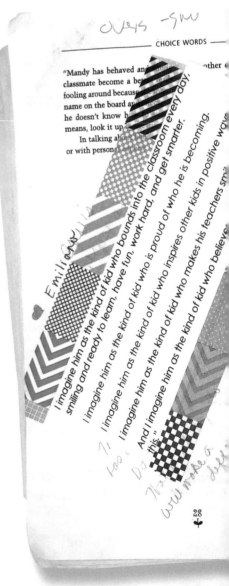

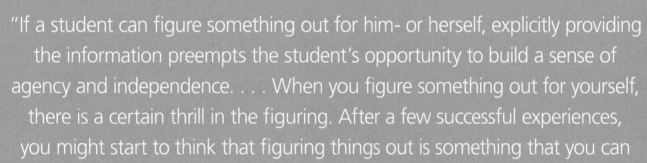

"If a student can figure something out for him- or herself, explicitly providing the information preempts the student's opportunity to build a sense of agency and independence. . . . When you figure something out for yourself, there is a certain thrill in the figuring. After a few successful experiences, you might start to think that figuring things out is something that you can actually do. Maybe you are even a figuring-out kind of person. . . . When you are told what to do, particularly without asking, it feels different. Being told what to do and how to do it—over and over again—provides the foundation for a different set of feelings and a different story about what you can and can't do, and who you are."

—PETER H. JOHNSTON, *CHOICE WORDS: HOW OUR LANGUAGE AFFECTS CHILDREN'S LEARNING*

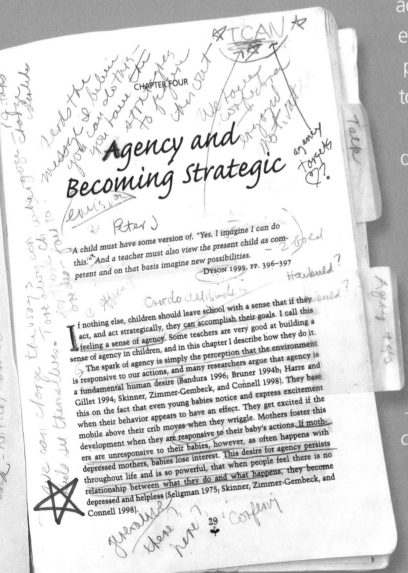

Peter Johnston's insights on agency

action, and work to place children in learning situations where they have daily opportunities to develop agency both as learners and as whole people.

I first learned the term *agency* from Peter Johnston in his book *Choice Words: How Language Affects Children's Learning* (2004). I've read that little green book again and again over the years, and every time I do, I find something new to wonder and think about.

Lately, when it comes to agency, I've been thinking about this: We can't *give* students agency. But we can give them the gifts of time, community, access, and choice, a clear vision of what they're working toward and why it matters, and one-on-one conferring so that agency can live and grow within them.

The word *agency* has an air of mystery about it. We may have a vague notion of what it means, though it's not something many of us talk about in the hall or the parking lot after school. But I wish it were.

Because I'm thinking agency is all about how we view ourselves as learners and doers, how we want others to view us, and eventually how we live our lives. Do we respond to challenging learning situations passively, or do we act with confidence and purpose? Are we helpless when trying or learning to do something new, or do we have a let-me-have-at-it kind of attitude? When we believe we have what it takes to figure out something that's within our reach, we set to work and engage, using what we know and doing what we can.

All true. But I find myself being and feeling all those things: sometimes I'm passive and sometimes I'm confident. Take writing, for instance. For me, it's hands-down hard, even though I've written books and articles before and have evidence that it's something I'm successful at. Even with all that, there are moments when I don't feel like I can figure out what to do to be successful; there are moments when I've lost my agency as a writer. But because I've come out on the other side of these feelings of frustration and self-doubt before, I have some strategies to help me.

For example, I can:

❖ set the timer for thirty minutes and write the whole time—no checking email, answering the phone, doing a load of laundry, watering a dead plant, or straightening up my writing area;

❖ scroll through photos of the four little girls I love most for inspiration;

❖ read;

How does this connect to Burkins & Yaris?

❖ email my editor, Margaret;

❖ leave it be for today, confident that I'll be refreshed and ready to have at it again the next morning; or

❖ take a walk or try to take a nap, because sometimes it's magical and the answers I'm searching for somehow manifest themselves.

When I feel I can't write, there are things I know to do to help me get back to "I can." By navigating that struggle, I'm reminding myself that I'm a writer and that the struggle is just part of, not the limitation of, my experience.

Agency transfers. Having agency around writing also gives me agency about other things, too. That's because I know what it's like to succeed at something, to feel proud because I struggled, worked hard, and finished something I cared about. It means that in many other areas where I can't yet do something, I might be able to, and that I can choose.

[handwritten margin note: We help students develop agency by giving them strategies to problem-solve & then stepping back & allowing the rdr. to p.s.]

What the Research Tells Us

Agency is the capacity and propensity to take purposeful initiative—the opposite of helplessness. Young people with high levels of agency do not respond passively to their circumstances; they tend to seek meaning and act with purpose to achieve the conditions they desire in their own and others' lives. The development of agency may be as important an outcome of schooling as the skills we measure with standardized testing. (Ferguson et al. 2015, 14)

[handwritten margin note: Post to review]

As adults, we've hopefully identified enough areas where we are agentive that we can apply what we've learned in new situations. Take a look at my bulleted list of agency strategies for writing again (below). How are some of these agency strategies transferable?

Strategies for Writing This Book

Set the timer for thirty minutes and write the whole time—no checking email, answering the phone, doing a load of laundry, watering a dead plant, or straightening up my writing area.

Scroll through photos of the four little girls I love most for inspiration. My granddaughters remind me of my life's purpose.

Read. Reading can give me new perspectives on what I'm writing about and replenish my intellectual resources. Sometimes, when I'm writing, I find unexpected and very specific inspiration in a book that has nothing to do with my topic.

Email or call Margaret, my editor.

Leave it be for today, confident that I'll be refreshed and ready to have at it again the next morning.

Take a walk or try to take a nap, because sometimes it's magical and the answers I'm searching for somehow manifest themselves.

Strategies for Agency

Transferrable Strategies for Agency

Work at the difficult task for a small, focused chunk of time.

Find outside inspiration, either directly related to the task or tangentially.

Temporarily disengage and focus on self-care. Before disengaging, set a time to return to the difficult task.

Talk to someone about the difficulty.

Our experiences with agency are never limited to the past tense: we're always facing new challenges that require us to access and expand our problem-solving strategies in order to feel and be successful. That's why I'm always asking children, "How did you figure that out? What exactly did you do?" This requires them to notice and name what they did, to think back and think out loud about the mental processes they've used to figure things out. The larger their problem-solving repertoires are, the more agentive, confident and capable they will be. When children experience confusion, I want them to think: "Okay. I don't get this. What do I know about what I can do to fix it? What strategy will I try first?" In time and through experience, children learn that this is a process they can trust.

Our language can help or hinder children's process

Children come to understand that difficulty is normal, that there are strategies they know and can use to address difficulty, and that they can overcome difficulty through effort. Not perfectly, but successfully. We get into trouble when we are so eager for students' success that we eliminate opportunities for struggle. When we do that, we're not being honest, we're sending the message that they can passively glide through their learning, learning should be easy, and smart people don't fail or struggle. Then children become disengaged because they know something's not right. They think that we don't believe they have what it takes to be successful. And even if they actually do the work, there's no satisfaction in it.

Our intentions are pure—we don't want children to become disheartened if something doesn't work. But that disheartenment can be a good thing—it can help us guide the child into another way of figuring things out. We say, "That strategy wasn't quite right for you this time, was it? Let's think. What else might you try?" If they're stuck, we offer a suggestion or two. In time they'll learn to become metacognitive about their own engagement in learning and take action. They'll come to understand that when things go awry, it's a natural consequence of learning and not a big deal. They learn to try something else and keep going.

Fisher's idea of productive struggle

What happens if we underscaffold a child and he's not successful? We work with the child to fix it. Everyone—every child in our readers' workshop, every teacher, every adult, every human—fails and is disengaged like Emiliano at some point. We need to expect (and appreciate!) this, and our behavior—the way we respond to children when it happens—has to demonstrate that. The best way I know to support children's sense of agency happens within the workshop structure.

Time for Agency.

- •Mini lesson•
  I will learn new strategies from my teacher to get smarter

- •Share•
  I will learn and share how we will get smarter.

- I will read, talk write/draw to get smarter and grow as a person

- •Independent work time•

- •Conferring•
  Renews energy and focuses on learner and teacher

What's the R.R. model for this?

Work time is where agency develops and grows—children need time to dig in and work hard to figure something out and learn something new.

There's a reason that two-thirds of workshop minutes are dedicated to independent work time. This is where agency flourishes: Imagine children reading, writing, drawing, and talking together to get smarter about reading and themselves as readers. They have their books, notebooks, pencils, markers, or whatever they need to figure things out and make meaning for themselves and each other. Their teacher has given them something to try, and they're working hard to apply it in ways that are unique to them. The teacher confers with them during this time, listening, giving feedback, and helping them set individual goals. Then during reflection and share time, children teach each other what they've learned about reading and themselves as readers.

Let's start to think about what that would mean for Emiliano.

▒ Imagining New Possibilities for a Child

I'm drawn to kids like Emiliano. Somehow they wriggle their way into my head and heart and never seem to leave. (There's quite a crowd in there after all these years!)

As a consultant in Emiliano's school, I have only five days in his classroom, but I'm determined to see whether I can find this little boy who isn't quite sure he wants to be found. At least not yet.

I need to view him in a different way—to get past what makes the relationship difficult and envision the child as truly capable, as someone who wants to learn and get smarter, and as someone who secretly, or maybe unconsciously, hopes his teacher will recognize the dreams that live within and see him for who he really is.

And so I wonder, "Could the conscious act of viewing a child as capable offer the promise of a new narrative? Does imagining possibilities make them more believable and doable?" I say yes! Because now we're focusing on what could happen instead of what is happening. We're thinking about the best that could happen, rather than the worst. But we all know that imagining alone won't make it so—it takes hard work too. But envisioning new possibilities for a child does mean that we are being generous and realistic enough to see a child as something more when he is in a moment of struggle—we are seeing who the child is, not who we (or a supervisor) wishes the child could be. As teachers, we hold onto that vision of possibility and make ourselves accountable enough to identify one realistic step for that child to take toward a more powerful identity today . . . and then another tomorrow . . . and then one the day after that.

And maybe, the child will imagine new possibilities for us, too.
And so I imagine new possibilities for Emiliano.

I imagine him as the kind of kid who bounds into the classroom every day, smiling and ready to learn, have fun, work hard, and get smarter.

I imagine him as the kind of kid who is proud of who he is becoming.

I imagine him as the kind of kid who inspires other kids in positive ways.

I imagine him as the kind of kid who makes his teachers smile.

And I imagine him as the kind of kid who believes, "Yes, I imagine I can do this."

Great quote to post

"When you change the way you look at things, the things you look at change."
—MAX PLANCK, PHYSICIST

We've been talking about one child, but we also want to take time to imagine possibilities for every child in our care. We don't have to do it all at once, or go down the class list, checking children off—we want to be open to the imagining. Maybe we notice that Charlotte always has her notebook with her, and when we look closely, her words sound like poetry. What might we imagine for her and with her? Or perhaps we spy Kevin out on the playground, gently mediating another dispute about the rules for King of the Mountain. What might be possible for him? It's the daily interactions with children that lend themselves to imagining possibilities. This is really part of long-term and daily planning. What do we want for them this year, this unit, this day, both individually and collectively? Then we think about how our teaching can help them get there.

To make the possibilities I imagine for Emiliano real, I need to help him develop new habits and routines that allow him to try on a *new* identity. I need to ensure his learning situations aren't too easy or too hard, but just right. He needs to be clear that his effort, his hard work, and the strategies he's using to figure things out are making him smarter. And even though I know he's smart, he needs to discover it for himself.

I'm ready.

But I have to find him first.

▨ Conferring to Support Access and Choice

Conferring with children is the most important work we do—every child deserves our one-on-one attention. It's also our most interesting work, sometimes the most challenging, and often the most fun. We never quite know what's going to happen or what a child will say. Conferences are as individual as the children we teach— when we pull up a chair next to a child, we remind ourselves that she is the most important one in the room right now. That focus reminds the child that the work is about her and her agency as a reader, learner, and person.

I look and look for Emiliano until finally I see him. He's curled up under a table, barricaded by pillows, doing I'm not sure what. I get down on my hands and knees, put my head under the table, and say, "There you are, Emiliano; I've been looking for you! Come on out and let's talk about what you're going to read and do today to get smarter about reading and yourself as a reader."

He doesn't budge. "So are you the kind of kid who's going to hide under the table, or are you the kind of kid who's going to work hard and share with every-one how you got smarter today?"

I wait. My back is killing me. And then, finally, he crawls out.

"Hi. That's just what I thought you'd do! Go get your book and let's see where you are." He does, and we do.

During our conference, I learn he's reading a book about the life cycle of butterflies. I ask him what he's learned so far, and if there are any words or ideas tripping him up. I find out he's interested in the topic, and though the text is challenging by traditional leveling standards, the photographs are accurate and beautiful, and we believe it's within his reach if he decides to work at it. (In other words, it's perfect!)

So we make a plan. But not just any plan—I need to make sure of two things:

1. *We make it our plan, not my plan.* I listen to his ideas—he thinks rereading a page at a time is what he needs to do. And while that wouldn't be *my* first choice for him, I'm going with it—I've listened, it's a viable plan, and it puts him in charge of his learning. Right now, this is about building relationships and letting him know I trust him. And hoping he's learning he can trust me.

2. *He knows just what he's going to do during work time and why it's important.* Near the end of the conference, I write his goal on a sticky note, along with the plan we've made, and leave it with him. His plan is to find a good spot; have his book, his pencil, and a pack of sticky notes at the ready; and read. We talk about how rereading might be a smart thing to try, and he decides to tally how many times he needs to reread a page in order to figure out all the words and read it fluently. "This is like doing research," I say. "Now you'll find out if rereading helps you grow as a reader." The implication: *This is what readers do to get ready to read and learn. I care about you and want you to be successful. And you're the one who gets to do the work and figure out how, or if, this strategy works for you.*

When Emiliano chose the butterfly book, I could have directed him back to the Butterfly tub and asked him to choose a "just-right" book, one that would be easier for him to read. But I didn't. Choice is an agentive act, and he'd taken a risk, spending time choosing this book out of all the others.

So now the choice is mine to make: Do I change the dynamic from him *wanting* to read a book to *having* to read a book? Or is there a way I can support him just enough so that he can be, and feel, truly successful?

What the Research Tells Us

According to John Guthrie and Nicole Humenick (2004), ensuring that students had access to an array of interesting texts produced reading achievement gains roughly four times as large as the small effect of providing systematic phonics instruction alone.

In addition, they found that providing students with choices about what to read, where to read, and with whom produced an impact on reading achievement more than three times as large as reported for systematic phonics instruction alone.

What Is a Just-Right Book?

Remember, the term *just right* is fluid—it depends on what children are working toward. As you help children choose, consider these questions:

(ADAPTED FROM MILLER AND MOSS 2013, 51.)

Could a book that's easy to read be just right for a child working on fluency?

Could a book above a child's level be just right for that child if he has extensive background knowledge about its content or is highly motivated to read it?

Could a book be just right for a child working on comprehension if the words are easy to read but the content is challenging?

Could a book be just right for a child working on decoding if she knows most of the words, but not all of them, and the content is easy to understand?

Could a challenging book be just right for the child who is highly motivated to read it?

Could a book that's easy to read be just right for the child who needs to build background knowledge for a specific topic?

So, I honor Emiliano's choice to continue with that butterfly book, but then we have to think together in our conference about what he's going to do with it. I ask him and he thinks rereading a page at a time is a good idea. I honor that choice, too, as an inquiry into strategies that work for him. Maybe it will help him in some ways and maybe he'll learn something about himself as a reader if it doesn't work, so we agree to that as today's inquiry for independent work time.

If rereading isn't helpful for Emiliano, we can talk about it. Nothing will be lost—investigating something you're interested in is never a waste of time. I might say, "It's such a good thing you did some research on this, Emiliano. What do you know now that you didn't know before?" The implication? *You're smarter now. You've figured out something about yourself as a reader.* And then, I can ask, "What do you want to try next?" The implication? *If one strategy doesn't work, try another one.*

If he doesn't have another strategy, I might say, "What about this? Hang on to the book you have, and go get a few more books about butterflies that you can easily read. I'm wondering whether building your background knowledge about butterflies with these new books will help you read your first one. You might even try reading them together. Want me to show you how that might look?" The implication? *I'm with you. I'll support you any way I can. Let's stick with this.*

[handwritten margin note: the process — Here's how we give students choice & help them build agency]

▩ Paying Attention During Independent Work Time

Independent work time is when we study how children work. How are they showing engagement or disengagement? How might a quick conversation help both the student and I better understand his learning and offer him some strategies to grow? If I only released students to complete a task, then they might just

What the Research Tells Us

In a study that identified twenty ways students spend instructional time, the only variable that explained gains on the posttest was time spent on actual text reading; time spent on other factors like phonemic awareness, word, or alphabetic instruction failed to predict improved achievement. (Miller and Moss 2013, 16–17)

How Do We Increase Stamina and Student Agency?

Ideas to Think About

For early readers, consider two independent reading sessions, ten to fifteen minutes each. In Rachel Brody's kindergarten class at Slavens Elementary in Denver, children come in, put their folders away, and find their way to the carpet, where every day there are a group of books spread out—one day might be alphabet books, another day wordless books, another day nonfiction. Children sit together in a circle and choose a book to read and interact with for ten to fifteen minutes. Rachel sits in the middle of the circle and confers with individuals and partners. Next up? Singing, maybe a little dancing, and a short morning meeting, followed by readers' workshop. Beautiful.

Work time isn't about head-in-a-book, silent reading. Think about what readers do in the worl—they read, write, and talk. Show students how and why.

Are their books worthy of what we are asking them to do? If kids have books that don't allow them to do this work, they'll be stuck.

Do they have a variety of books they are interested in? Early readers need ABC books, songbooks, wordless books, rhyming books, and beginning readers in their stacks. All readers need fiction, nonfiction, and poetry, in all their variations. No limits!

Do children have a clear vision of what they're going to get smarter about today? Do they understand why they're doing what we've asked them to do?

It's not as much about the minutes as it is about the books! Put away the timer and the "growing our stamina, minute by minute" charts. When we focus on minutes, kids do, too. When children have books in their hands that they are interested in, that they can read, and that give them ideas to think and talk about, five minutes blur into ten, ten into fifteen, and more.

view the work as an act of compliance, but through my observation behaviors—watching, taking notes, conferring that focuses on listening, and ending work time by sharing what children noticed through their independent work time—I let them know that independent work time is a time for discovery and that the work they're doing is the vehicle for discovery; it's secondary to the process. For children who, like Emiliano, show signs of disengagement or struggle such as not reading, pretending to read, wandering around the room, tapping their pencil, playing with something from home, and so on, I seek them out right away. If it's one or two children, I meet with them individually; if it's three or four, I bring them together in a small group. (And if it's more than that, I need to rethink my lesson—it's obviously me, not them!)

I tell them that I've noticed they're having some trouble getting started, or sticking with it, and ask, "How can I help?" or, "What do you need?" Maybe I'll learn they didn't understand what to do, their book isn't a good match, they're not feeling well, or they're missing their dad, who is out of town. Whatever it is, we do our best to fix it, we come up with a plan, and back out they go. I check back in five minutes or so to see how things are going.

We increase time spent reading on subsequent days, depending on what we're noticing. As soon as things show signs of falling apart—kids getting restless, asking "How much longer do we have?" and so on—I call everyone back to reflect and share.

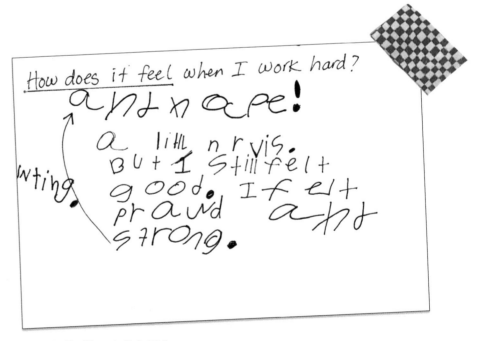

Emiliano's Exit Ticket

At the end of independent work time, Emiliano has clear evidence that he's smarter than he was in the beginning, and he knows just how he did it, as shown on his exit ticket. Emiliano is smarter when he finishes. He can read three pages that he couldn't read before, and he can teach others about what he learned about himself as a reader. And he's close to discovering that rereading helps him not only learn new words but also remember what he's read. The implication: *The more I work, the smarter I get.*

Dear Reader, I loved reading this response from Emiliano—the fact that he used the words **good**, **proud**, **strong**, and **happy** to describe how he felt made me feel proud, too. Proud of him, for sure, and also proud of myself—I stayed mindful and calm, and it paid off.

And I also loved his honesty when he wrote he felt "a little nervous." Again, I thought, "Me, too." Sometimes we feel unsure about how to begin. We wonder, "What will be best for this child?" I started slowly with Emiliano, asking him if he'd take a few books back to the library and making sure to thank him when he returned. The message? **I trust you to leave the classroom and come back.** When I noticed him working, I nodded, smiled, and sometimes asked, "How's it going?" The message? **I'm noticing your hard work. I see you.** Not in an "I'm watching you" kind of way, but in an "I'm noticing and I believe in you" way.

When I sent my own children off to school, I wanted them to learn and be successful. But even more, I hoped their teachers would take the time to get to know them, to care about them, to understand and appreciate the little boys we loved so much.

I try to remember that. Emiliano, and all children, have moms, dads, and families who need us to appreciate and love their sons and daughters too.

–Debbie

Emiliano has gotten smarter today, both as a reader and as a learner. Is he now, in just five days, the kind of kid who thinks, "Yes, I imagine I can do this"? Not yet. But he's closer this day than he was the day before.

Yes, he has a long way to go, but this isn't about mastery. It's about approximation, and becoming, and believing in himself enough to experiment, to take some risks and try something out, to stretch himself a bit and see what he can learn. Every day he gets a little smarter, learns a little more, and begins to believe that maybe, just maybe, he is that kind of kid.

And that's our responsibility to children: we put a child in learning situations that are just beyond his reach—the kind that, with a little support from us and a little struggle from the child, will help him be successful, once, twice, and again and again and again.

And just imagine the possibilities for Emiliano—and his classmates—in five weeks, five months, and five years. There are often issues that get in the way of establishing enough trust to talk with a child about his or her learning, but overcoming those obstacles (even if we have to crawl halfway under a table!) is the essence of our work. If we can continue to show up, teach, and develop the spark of agency within the children we teach, we'll show them how to get smarter about themselves, how to learn, how to live, and maybe even how to love.

"Smart isn't something you are. Smart is something that you get."

—JEFF HOWARD,
EFFICACY INSTITUTE

You might be wondering, "But what if he hadn't crawled out from under the table? What then?"

Well first off, dragging him out from under the table wouldn't be something I'd have considered. (And I doubt you would, either!) Neither would I have written his name on the board, sent him to the office, or denied him recess. He was not hurting anyone, and any one of these options would have further escalated the situation and put us right back where we were before.

Instead, I'd have said something like this: "Emiliano, I need to confer with Angel and Mara. When you're ready, get your books, and find a good spot to start reading." The implication: *This decision is yours to make; you're the one with the power. I'm getting back to business.* I'd have been giving him a vision of how he could make things right—get his books and start reading. Low-stakes, win-win for both of us. (And we can talk about this hiding thing another time, thinking together about why and how we could make things better.)

What the Research Tells Us

No matter how well you plan and structure learning tasks, it's the one-on-one interactions [with children] that inform the power and effectiveness in your teaching. (Fountas and Pinnell 2017, 1)

 ## Conferring to Inquire and to Offer Community

The structure of conferring sets up an expectation that students have been doing something worthy in their independent work time. I walk over to a child, excited to find out what that child is thinking about. Part of it may be struggle, but there's going to be something important in that struggle that, if attended to, might help not only that child but the entire community of readers in that classroom, and so I invite the child to share.

Conferring is a moment for fixing our assumptions about what we imagine a child is doing. Sometimes we assume more or less is going on with a child than is actually happening, and truly we can't rely on our assumptions to assess children's learning. Conferring grounds us in reality. Without that daily practice, we risk stumbling upon our own fears and fantasies. Through conferring, we recognize not only where the child is but also where we are, and take the opportunity to refocus on reality.

At the end of my five days in Emiliano's classroom, I wanted to make sure to check in with him. I went to where I'd seen him last, and though his books were there, he wasn't. I spotted him huddled in a corner with a permanent marker and whole pack of sticky notes and found myself shaking my head. "What's he doing?" I wondered, feeling somehow betrayed and thinking that whatever it was, it couldn't be good. I took three deep breaths and headed over. "So what's up?" I asked. He gave me a shy smile, lined up four sticky notes on the file cabinet nearby, and explained, pointing to each one:

"This is me reading.

"This is me reading more. See how my brain is getting bigger?

"And now I'm reading more and more and I'm getting smarter and smarter! See how big my brain is now?

"It's a little book. And here's the title. Can I share it?"

"Oh, Emiliano," I said. "Of course you can share. Putting all that effort into reading your books really is making you smarter. Can you share with everyone what you do as a reader now that you didn't do before?"

Emiliano's book to share

He looks at me, smiles, and nods.

Conferring is one of the ways we help children understand that even when they're working alone, they're not alone in their work. When we confer, we show we're interested in what they are doing and that their work is interesting and relevant enough to share with others.. We invite children to share their thinking and learning, keeping their focus on what they learned about themselves as readers, rather than their reading. This highlights the processes children use to make meaning and figure things out, serving not only the child who is sharing, but also giving others something new to think about or try.

Here are other questions we might ask children to discuss during share time:

❖ How did work time feel today? What made it feel that way?

❖ What did you learn about yourself as a reader today?

❖ Why are we spending our time learning how to do this? Why does it matter?

❖ Is there something you tried today that you think you will do tomorrow and in the days and weeks to come? Is there something you're still thinking about?

❖ Did you have any problems today? What did you do?

❖ What goal(s) will you set for yourself tomorrow?

When we ask questions like these, we're going for conversations, not isolated comments. We facilitate that in the beginning with questions like, "What does someone else think about that?" and children gradually assume more and more responsibility for these reflective share-time discussions, and at the same time advance the collective sense of agency. Here it's about children coming together, reflecting and teaching each other what they've learned, how they did it, and why they believe it matters. So now it's not so much about "I'm the kind of kid who can figure things out" as it is collectively "*We're* the kind of kids who can figure things out."

The previous questions are those I most often ask children, but they hold true for us, too. What if we chose one of these to think about every day?

❖ How did work time feel today? What made it feel that way?

❖ What did I learn about myself as a teacher today?

❖ Why does the work I'm asking children to do matter?

❖ What did I learn or do today that I want to keep doing?

❖ What was problematic today? How will I fix it?

❖ How hard did I work to get smarter about my students today? What are my goals for myself tomorrow?

post for me to consider

▨ Postscript

I went back to Emiliano's school to visit the following year. I met a lot of the children I'd worked with the previous year, but (wouldn't you know) Emiliano had moved to another school. And so I wrote the following manifesto (as if he'd written it) to all the teachers he'll have in the years to come—it's my love letter to him and so many kids just like him.

Things changed for both of us over those five days. Emiliano was on his way. He was becoming more literate and developing an agentive stance, right in front of his (and everyone else's) very own eyes. Now he saw himself as the kind of kid who was getting smarter and smarter, the kind of kid whose brain was getting bigger and bigger, *and he knew it was because of his own efforts.* He was the author of a new story about himself, and though I'll never know what happened next, I remain hopeful that he continued to feel proud, and strong, and happy.

Emiliano's Manifesto

Make sure the work you ask me to do is challenging enough to help me grow.

Give me time. Notice and praise my effort and hard work, and ask me to explain the strategies I used to figure things out.

Support me, but let me find my way.

Please don't feel sorry for me—your sympathetic smile and eyes become an excuse for us both.

Please don't overscaffold me, no matter how much you want to, or how many times I say, "I don't want to," or "I can't." This is not good for me. Believe in me and help us both understand that a little struggle is a good thing.

Help me understand that when I fail, you're not worried, and I shouldn't be either. What's important for me is to stick with it. Show me possibilities.

Show me that you care about me and that you'll always be in my corner.

Believe in me, no matter what. Know that sometimes you have to believe in me first, before I can believe in you, or myself.

Let me know you love me. (I'll love you back.)

23

Whoever is doing
the reading, writing,
and talking is doing
the thinking.
—SAM BENNETT

The biggest growth in my teaching life
has been acts of removal. Less of my
voice. Less of my needs. Less of my
personality. I aim to be a steady and
supportive background presence.
—KRISTINE MRAZ, @MRAZKRISTINE

CHAPTER 2

What If We Made What Children Make and Do Our Priority?

Finding Our Way to a Beautiful Question: Workshop Planning

Some years back, my friend Sam Bennett, an amazing educator and literacy coach, challenged me to get smarter about readers' workshop. She always provokes deep thinking—either directly or through her practice—and every now and again I honestly wonder if I'm up to the task. But Sam believes I am, so I do, too. (I wish all teachers a Sam!)

On this particular day, we were busy at my kitchen table, planning the first of a series of lessons for some upcoming work. Once we'd identified the learning target, I began looking through the stack of books we'd gathered, getting ready to think through the minilesson. But Sam shifted my attention to work time—she was thinking about what kids would read, write, and talk about instead. I was surprised and intrigued. We were planning work time before planning the lesson? I decided to put myself in the moment and see what I could learn.

My head was spinning when Sam left—here I thought I knew all about workshop and now I was wondering if I'd been wrong all along. I knew deep down this wasn't really true, but this is how we can feel (especially early on) when we question something we believe we know really well.

For the next couple of days (and, um, nights), I kept thinking about our planning session and wondering: "Why *am* I doing this particular thing in this particular way?" This wasn't about the big ideas of workshop—time, choice, response, and community; the particular thing I was thinking about was how I *planned* for workshop.

Sometimes we do things without really thinking about why—it just *is*. But when we challenge ourselves with the question, "Why am I doing this particular thing in this particular way?" we're acknowledging that we need to take time to reflect, rethink, and maybe even revitalize our teaching. *And ourselves.*

Tom Newkirk writes:

> *If we are honest with ourselves, it is not always external forces that inhibit us. We can all be victims of our own inertia when we feel passive and mediocre and tired—so that even the thought of making a change and investigating it feels like too much effort. We are in a rut, we are settling, we are not the teacher we want to be. At moments like this the action of research is not an additional burden; it is the way up and out. (2016, 9)*

He explains that teacher research doesn't have to be imposing and intimidating. It's not always about finding one truth, but can sometimes instead be about opening up possibilities and pulling us out of unproductive routines.

He describes the cycle of true research as this: *Take something you think you know, and through sustained attention, begin to see it anew.*

The structure I know best for teaching and learning is workshop. I've been at it for years now, and it's a big part of who I am and what I talk about and do in my current work with teachers and children. And now I was giving it my sustained attention yet again, thinking about planning for workshop in new ways. Prioritizing work time felt important, interesting, and at the same time challenging, so to get started, I decided to begin with what drove the focus of my current daily lesson planning: the learning target.

Learning targets identify what all children will get smarter about each day. Unlike teacher objectives, learning targets are written for children—they identify a chunk of learning that's written in kid-friendly language, measurable, and rooted in standards and content. You may not use learning targets, but you likely plan around a standard, a teaching point, or a focus. So even if you don't use them, stay with me a minute, because thinking about them helped me get where I needed to

go. Learning targets are most often written as "I can" or "We can" statements, as in, "I can explain the strategies I use to help me remember new learning."

I think I jumped into planning the minilesson after identifying the learning target because that's the way I'd always done it: Plan the target. Plan the lesson. Plan work time. But here's the question from Sam that inspired me to reconsider what I'd been doing: "How will you know what children will need you to show or teach them (in a minilesson) until you figure out what they will *do* during those thirty to forty minutes of work time—what will children read, write (make), and talk about in order to get smarter about the target?"

Once I began planning work time before the minilesson, I realized pretty quickly that I'd been spending much more time and energy planning lessons than I had planning what children would read, write, and talk about during work time. My minilessons were driving readers' workshop; I'd made them my

Do we plan work time in RR?

most important consideration. Once I figured that out and it roiled around in my head awhile, I came to understand I really had been going about things backward—I'd been prioritizing my minilessons when I should have been prioritizing children's work time! (I remember thinking, "How could this be? How did I not grasp this big idea ages ago?" But then I thought about my ongoing pledge to be kind to myself, and I reminded myself what I always tell others: "When we know better, we do better." Thank you, Maya Angelou, for those wise words.)

When we plan work time first, children are the ones driving our workshops *and* our planning—we're planning for what they will read, write, and talk about first and *then* we're planning for what they will need from us (in a minilesson) in order to be successful. This way, work time (and children) becomes our priority, and minilessons take on a new, ancillary role—they serve to *support* children in their efforts, giving them just what they need to figure things out for themselves. And now, along with Sam, I'm the one doing the advocating: Plan the target. Plan the work time. Plan the minilesson.

Take a look at readers' workshop structure based on time.

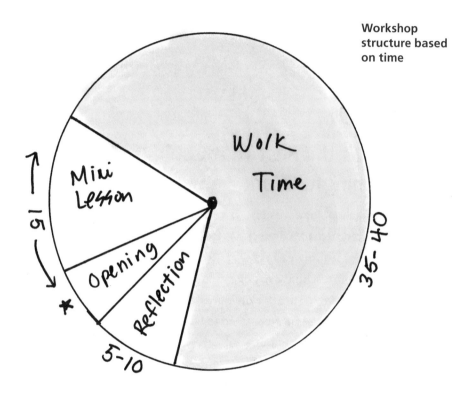

Workshop structure based on time

Wow, right? Seeing that big block of time (and the number of minutes) for kids to read, write, and talk helped me understand then—and reinforces now—why planning work time for children must be my first priority. It contains the most minutes and is the most significant feature of workshop—this is where kids are digging in, reading, writing, talking, and learning about reading and themselves as readers. The premise (and the promise) for children and teachers is this: Everyone can do this. Everyone can get smarter every day. Everyone deserves to feel sixty minutes smarter after a sixty-minute readers' workshop. And everyone deserves at least one year of growth. Let's look at how we can keep our promise to deliver that growth through the structure of workshop.

"Human nature has been sold short. . . . [Humans have] a higher nature which . . . includes the need for meaningful work, for responsibility, for creativeness, for being fair and just, for doing what is worthwhile and for preferring to do it well."

—ABRAHAM MASLOW,
EUPSYCHIAN MANAGEMENT: A JOURNAL

What's the Best That Could Happen? Meaningful Work

We call it "workshop" for a reason; the learning time is about the work children do. Children need to make connections from one day's learning to the next; it's the story of their meaningful work and the how, what, and why of their learning, not the story of our teaching. I'm not thinking about heads-down, nose-to-the-grindstone kind of work; I'm after the kind of work that fuels children from one day to the next, work that inspires them to want to read more, write more, talk more, learn more, understand more, and grow.

Meaningful work is worthwhile, interesting, I-want-to-find-out kind of work—that's why I always seem to be asking children, teachers, and most of all myself, "Why does doing this work matter? Why are we spending our time doing this, anyway?" We all need to be clear about why so that we can create learning situations where children will engage and come to understand why it matters too.

It's not easy work—that would be tedious and a waste of children's time. Sometimes kids don't know why what we're asking them to do matters, and don't even act like they want to know, at least not yet. Meet nine-year-old Sasha. She's lying down, head on a pillow, with a book about fossils open and covering her face. I spot her name tag and say, "Hi, Sasha. What's going on over here? Can we talk?" She sits up and tells me she's bored and she doesn't like her book and she's tired and she doesn't know why she has to talk to me since I'm not her real teacher.

The learning target for Sasha and her class is this: *We can explain the strategies we use to help us remember new learning.* I did a think-aloud to show how I make connections from new learning to what I already know to help me remember

Texcher Box

de Cato?
to Cato

Give them
A eleent
And piggy
Book.

Atime 2'

list o

Top of
yarn

31

what I'm learning, and I encouraged children to try it out—I told them this was going to be like research, and for the next couple of weeks they'd be learning about themselves and each other and what they do to remember important information.

But my enthusiasm obviously hasn't resonated with Sasha. The first thing we do is to try to find another book, and surprisingly she lights up when she sees a book about squirrels. We talk about what she knows—she has ideas about what they eat, and she learns more as she reads. I refer back to the lesson, reminding her how she might want to connect her new learning to what she knows: she knew they ate nuts, and now she's learned they also eat pinecones, fruit, and seeds. She complies. But still, I get the feeling she's acquiescing just to please me. Sasha is "doing school." I leave her, wondering what she'll do next. I stand back to observe, watching as she jams the squirrel book back in the tub and throws her sticky notes into the trash.

It's frustrating, especially because we're always yearning for those miracle moments we hear and read about. But this kind of disengagement is real, and we can't pretend that all of us won't encounter it. What we're seeing here in this moment is the truth about how Sasha sees herself as a reader—she throws her work away because she doesn't think it has value or that she has value as a reader. I need to know that in order to figure out what makes the most sense for Sasha next. Seeing the truth of how children view our teaching and their learning, *and* identifying a logical next step to support them, *is* the best that can happen for work time.

Teaching isn't really about miracles. Teaching is about hard work, building relationships, establishing trust, and sticking with it. Part of helping children take on the work of real learning is helping them recognize but not get defeated by the inevitable struggle of learning. Every reader will feel disengaged, defeated, angry, sad, and frustrated by learning. That's something we can count on. And children need to count on us to help them understand that struggle isn't a sign that they're not smart or that they're diminished in any way. Struggle is a sign that they need a little more time and an entry point into what they don't understand. With just the right amount of scaffolding, children will be able to do the work on their own and get better at it.

Today during work time, I have learned something about Sasha as a reader, and tomorrow, she'll be my first priority during work time. When we confer, I'm not going to pretend that today didn't happen or trick myself into believing that it was just a bad day. So I won't jump right into working with her about our learning target—teachers can "do school" too. When we do school, we forge ahead, forgetting that we teach children first, content second.

Instead, I'll start by telling her the truth. I'll let her know that I've been thinking about her since yesterday and ask her what she needs from me and how we can work together to make things better. She may not know yet, or even tell me if she does, but it's the asking that's important. She needs to know I believe in her, that I value her for who she is and not what she can do. The doing will come.

I know, too, that I need to give her some choices about new strategies to try—I need to do my best to place her in learning situations where she will come to understand for herself why the work we're asking her to do matters. We'll figure this out together—remember Emiliano and his tallying strategy? And though it's not really magic, listening, trusting, and believing in children can feel magical, in a real kind of way. This really is the best that could happen; we learn what we need to know to make sure no child slips through the cracks. It's always two connected questions: What is? And, based on that, what's next?

▨ Planning for What Children Will Do First

When we plan for work time, we ask: "What will children do to get smarter *post at my table* tomorrow? What will they read, write, and talk about?"

What will they read that's worthy of what we're asking them to do? We need to ensure children's books will allow them to practice what it is we're working toward. Some days children's choices are necessarily guided so they can do the work—if we're learning about narrative nonfiction, everyone needs to have at least one book of that genre. We gather as many as we can and they make their choices from these. (Children always have free-choice books in their stacks, too, but some days we need to supplement them with others that allow them to do the work and be successful.)

I teach children to think about these questions when choosing books:

❧ Does this book look interesting me? Do I want to read it?

❧ Can I read most of the words and understand most of the ideas? If I can't, do I have strategies I can use to access this text?

❧ Do I think it will give me something to think and talk about?

How do kids know if their book will give them something to talk about? Generally, if the book is truly interesting to the child, talking will happen, particularly if we're modeling it ourselves. We might say things like, "I've been reading this book about elephants, and I really want to talk about it. . . . Did you know . . . ?" Or maybe it's a big idea we can't figure out, or we have a question about a character. When we do this regularly, children will, too. We're helping them become aware of their reading, their thinking, and what fascinates them; we're helping them become interesting people who have interesting things to talk about.

What will they talk about *during work time that will allow them to deepen their understanding of the target and themselves (and each other) as readers and thinkers?* Talking in the midst of doing is optimal—things are fresh in their minds and they can process with someone about what is or isn't working, what mental processes they're using to make meaning, and of course, books and ideas.

Peter Johnston says language "actually creates realities and invites identities" (2004, 9). So when children talk about their learning, they're saying, *I am a learner.* When children talk about their reading, they're saying, *I am a reader.* When children talk about ideas, they're saying, *I am someone who cares about ideas and knows things.* And when children talk about their peers' reading and learning, they're saying, *I am someone who can learn from and care about the lives of others.* This is the kind of talk we plan for—we invite children to talk in these ways so they can continue to build their reading identities.

What the Research Tells Us

If you practice elaboration, there's no known limit to how much you can learn. Elaboration is the process of giving new material meaning by expressing it in your own words and connecting it with what you already know. The more you can explain about the way your new learning relates to your prior knowledge, the stronger your grasp of the new learning will be. . . . [Cognitive growth is] more likely when one is required to explain, elaborate, or defend one's position to others as well as to oneself; striving for an explanation often makes a learner integrate and elaborate knowledge in new ways. (Brown, Roediger, and McDaniel 2014, 3)

Here are some notes I took when listening in to a small group of children immersed in an author study of Chris Van Allsburg; they were intent on developing "theories" about him and the books he writes, and imagining how they might introduce him to someone who didn't know him or his books:

Ali: So how does he do it? How does he make us want to read his books so much? He makes me curious; he makes me want to read all his books.

Elijah: Me too! But every book is so weird, like in *Two Bad Ants*, all these ants are looking for this amazing crystal . . .

Aram: Wait, Elijah! I've read that one—I know what that amazing crystal is! You won't believe it when you find out!

Ali: But that's what he does to us! It's kind of like a trick, but a really good trick. Because you just can't believe you didn't know.

Aram: So is that a theory? He makes something we know feel like something we don't know?

Elijah: We should write that down. Let's look at *The Wretched Stone* and see if happens in that book, too. . . .

Ali, Elijah, and Aram are using language to create realities and invite identities. They're developing theories about an author; they see themselves as readers, learners, and kids who love to think and grapple with big ideas.

What the Research Tells Us

Talk helps children understand that meaning-making is not a matter of getting the right answer, because they quickly learn how different people make different, yet similar sense. In addition, the more they get to have such personal conversations with their classmates, the more they know them, and the less they are able to view them through stereotypes or to put them down. Stereotype and domination are made possible by reducing the complexity of others to the handful of features that mark them as different—as not-me. (Johnston 2004, 71)

Claire's note to Jake illustrates that Jake's thinking isn't just an artifact of his learning; it's his contribution to the community. His learning has a purpose and value to others. They need him, Claire explains, even though Jake might not realize it yet. And Claire, by her noticing of Jake, is demonstrating some agency of her own. She's showing that she knows what's valuable and that she has the power to support another child in sharing his value with the community. Are Claire and Jake much more likely to continue to be people who are not just intellectually curious about ideas in books but also curious and caring about the lives of others? Yes! By positioning their literacy within a community of readers, we help children understand their full agency as readers. It's not just about getting smarter, but about being more connected to and support-ive of others. That's how reading, writing, and talking can accomplish more than the learning target we've planned for the day.

From Claire's point of view, once we get to know a person well, we nudge him forward! (Talk does that.)

Jake—

you're a briliante reader and people love your thinking so much but you're too shy to share with others and so get over being shy and share your amazing thinking with others to get smarter!

-Claire

After a talking session I sometimes ask questions like these: "Are you smarter after your conversation with your partner or group? If so, how? What do you understand now that you didn't understand before? What's something new you might try?" Or, "What are you thinking about now that you weren't thinking about before?" Conversations like these broaden children's perspectives and pave the way for new thinking, insights, and ideas.

What do questions like these have in common?

- ❖ There's an emphasis on asking children to name how they learn things: I learned this, and this is how I learned it.

- ❖ They are open-ended and encourage a variety of perspectives: We are all growing and getting smarter.

- ❖ They imply that learning is a social act. Coming together to talk and think about big ideas and things that matter encourages the spirit of collaboration and the collective sense of agency: We are the kind of kids who can figure things out.

- ❖ The questions assume there is more than one teacher in the room: We are all teachers.

What are teachers doing during all this talking? We're getting smarter too! We're learning about how children are making sense of the target and about the effectiveness of our teaching. We're up and about, present, actively engaged, and learning as much as we can. Clipboards or notebooks in hand, we're observing, listening, taking notes, and considering feedback and implications for subsequent whole-group lessons, individual conferences, small-group work, and reflection and share time. The one thing we're not doing much of? Talking. Because right now, this isn't about us.

We can discover the strategies we
use to help us remember new learning.
Listening in —

Mason — Earthquakes — he's using his
body + hands to explain how earthquakes
begin — shakes his body — uses hand's to
mimic plates — And show types of
faults! (Share)

Emma —
Just sitting —
"I'm putting my
learning in my own
words" —

Jade —
squid —
schema — squirt
ink

new — speedy and
smart

tell it / I remember it

Read it
Take notes
Remember it —
Seth

Jocelyn —
I reread like 4
times until I
can close the
book and still say it"

Strategies Kids Use
(CHART THIS!
Ongoing)

○ Act it out
○ Visualize
○ talk about it w/ someone
○ make connections
○ draw
○ reread
○ take my time — merge pics/words

Benny —
I take my time
+ put together
what I learn
from the pics
and the
words

Take a look at my listening-in notes from Sasha's class. In just ten minutes, I have seven minilesson ideas, all from kids!

What will they write, draw, or create *that will give them and us concrete evidence of how they're getting smarter?* Although we'd love to, we can't possibly confer with every child every day. Asking children to make something concrete (most often something they write or draw) serves as a formative assessment and gives us, and them, yet another piece of evidence (along with conferring, listening in, and observation) of where individual children are and what they need next. Now we have something from every child to guide us as we plan for tomorrow. When we think about what children will make, we're identifying formative assessments, finding out where children are—we're finding out how they are approaching or meeting the learning target. Here are some examples.

Target: I can ask questions to help make meaning.

My name Malin

the Chick and the Duckling

can ask questions in stories to help me make meaning.

My name Asim

My book Rob Get In

I can ask questions in stories to help me make meaning.

Dad come bown Jad Went.

Dad Rob. FLeL bown.

BruL.

Yes!

Rob. Went bown.

My name Enzo

My book The Magic Fish

I can ask questions in stories to help me make meaning.

why H esWife is Bea meehn te The man?

why is The Prince a fish?

whx didn't you make a wish?

Why Dos it He wat to go back to a Hemaehe?

Why Dos it He wife Do the Wishis?

My name Zara

My book Fox and his friends

I can ask questions in stories to help me make meaning.

the charcter is fox.

Why is a fox skerd?

wer did sistr go? foxs

wrck first fun later.

why not is fox ther?

How do we keep track of, and learn from, all those sticky notes? Here, children recorded questions on sticky notes, placing them in their texts as they read. Near the end of work time they transferred the sticky notes to "thinking sheets." This keeps their sticky notes all together, and at the end of the day we can spread them out, giving teachers and children concrete evidence of where individual children are with this strategy, particularly when combined with conferring and listening in to student talk.

In these examples, two children are on their way, and I need to confer with the other two tomorrow. Did Robbie not have any questions in his book? Did he have questions, but not write them down? Or did he actually write his questions but forget to transfer them? I can't know until I confer with him tomorrow. And I'll also need to confer with Aiden tomorrow. This child needs more support with asking questions—I'm wondering if the text he's reading is worthy of the task? I'll bring along a book we've read aloud and maybe a wordless book to help me find out.

When thinking through what children will make, I ask questions like these:

Robbie: I can explain how I got smarter as a reader and about the topic. The "make" exit ticket

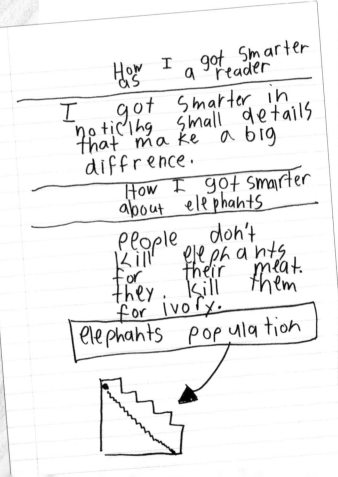

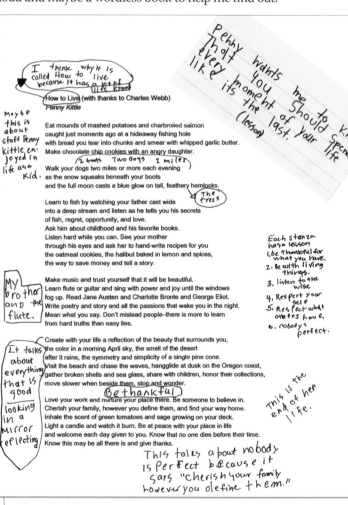

Aiden: I can determine importance in a poem. The "make" annotations on poem

❖ Is there a match between the learning target and what children will make? Will what they do or make give them and me clear evidence of where they are now and where they need to go?

❖ Is the target worthy of their time and effort? Why does doing this matter?

❖ Is it authentic work? Is it similar to what readers in the world think about and do?

❖ Does it focus on thinking? Does it require children to dig deep and think about things that matter to them?

❖ Is it open-ended? Will everyone have a seat at the table?

When you look closely at each child's "make" in the figures, notice how each one is taking ownership of his or her learning, as well as how they are approaching or meeting their learning target. Each artifact demonstrates to the child (and the teacher) that he or she has taken something important away from his or her interactions with the text that he or she can hold

Daniel: I can infer big ideas to help me make meaning. The "make" child's picture and words

Hector: I can identify the important message in a story. The "make" drawing

Riley: I can build my background knowledge about fairy tales to help me make predictions when I read. The "make" writing on paper

onto beyond this day's learning. These "makes" strengthen children's sense of agency—their work is evidence that they're the kind of kids who can do things.

Sometimes we ask children to make something without asking ourselves why—we're supposed to have a formative assessment and we rush to make something up, or we use something we've found somewhere that seems to fit. But does it really? Will it give you the information you'll need to help you plan for tomorrow? If the answer is no, or you're not sure, don't ask children to do it. It's better they read.

The thing we want to avoid most is busywork. This turns children off, and rightly so. We want to make sure what we ask children to do is authentic, purposeful, and worthy of their time and effort .

Planning for What Teachers Will Do During Work Time

As you might imagine, classrooms where children are encouraged to read, talk, and write about things that matter are not silent. But they're not loud, either. They're humming with children's voices—their ideas, questions, thinking, and learning. They're joyful, creative, friendly, and happy places, where children and

teachers learn and get smarter together. As children work independently, the teacher pays attention to the class as a whole during work time, observing (kid-watching), listening in to their conversations, conferring, and bringing together small groups of children when necessary, all to celebrate, navigate difficulty, and plan for what will come next in children's learning.

We are as intentional as we plan for what *we* will do during work time as we are when we plan for what children will do. Four teacher actions I want to plan for every day are kidwatching, conferring, listening in, and bringing together small groups.

I remind myself to stand back and notice (kidwatch) several times during work time, almost always at the beginning, and maybe a time or two later on. In just those few minutes I gain a sense of how things are going, who is doing what, who appears to be engaged, who doesn't, and more. Here are a few examples of the kinds of things I notice and the actions I might take:

❧ *Some kids don't seem to have their books out.* Kids need their books during readers' workshop! I'll wait it out for a short while to see if they resolve the problem themselves, but if not, it's my responsibility to find out why and what the children (or the children and I) can do to get a book they care about in their hands.

❧ *In general, kids seem confused.* This one's all on me—what did I forget to explain or model? In this situation, I might call everyone

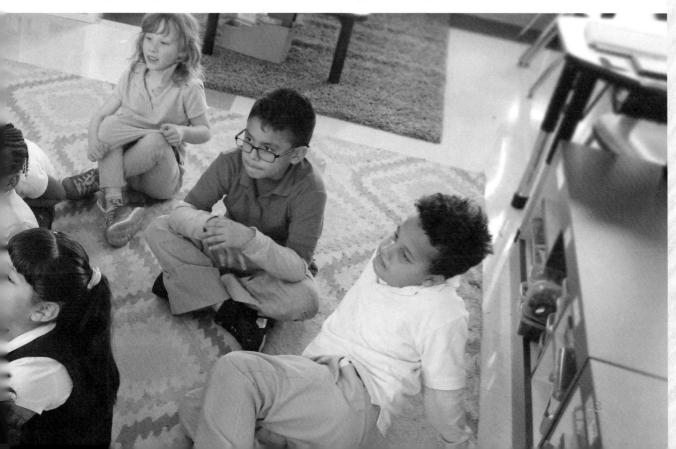

together or talk with them right where they are. If I'm unclear about why they are confused, I ask them. I clear up the confusion, letting them know I own it and I'm sorry. Then we're back at it.

❧ *A child doesn't seem like himself.* I need to find out why. Is he not feeling well? Is he sad? Angry? Is there anything I can do to help? If there is, I do it.

❧ *Almost everyone seems engaged, but something's going on over in the corner.* I need to find out what's happening, but I don't jump to conclusions—it just might be amazing.

❧ *One or more children seem to be having difficulty.* I check in with the child individually, or if there are more, I bring them together in a small group. I let them know what I've noticed, and ask them, "What do you need from me? How can I help?"

These quick observations help me see the big picture and address what needs to be addressed quickly. It keeps me present and aware of what's happening in real time. These observations help me decide whom I need to confer with right away, and, if there are ongoing patterns, it helps me understand what I can do better, whether it's my instruction or my relationships with children. Children aren't conscious of what I'm doing; I'm not at the front of the room with a clipboard, monitoring for compliance. This noticing is really just for me, to help me understand what's working and what isn't—it mostly serves to inform my teaching and my practice.

It's during *conferring*, not the minilesson, where our most significant teaching occurs—conferring is hands down the best way to find out where children are and what they need. It's a time to pull up a chair next to a child, slow things down, and personalize our teaching through listening, reflecting on what they say, and figuring out on the spot, often in real time in our notebooks, what they need most from us this day. It's about thinking and learning together—conferences are personal and friendly, and every one is different. Our minilessons are necessarily broad (there's no way we can meet the needs of all kids here), but conferences are specific to the child sitting by our side. This is where we differentiate our instruction and support children as readers. At the end of a conference, the child and I are smarter than at the beginning. The child, about reading and herself as a reader; me, about the child and where she needs to go next. I'm asking myself, "What do I know about this child? What do I know about reading? What do I know about myself as a reader?" And then I give it my best shot.

I use a notebook both to track my observations about individual children (jotted down just after we've finished our time together) and also to think through teaching points I know I want to use with individual children.

I also *listen in to student conversations.* As kids talk, I'm off to the side, listening in. I'm an observer now, going from small group to small group, or partnership to partnership, trying my best to write their words as I hear them and name them when I can. When I look at my notes later in the day, I learn about individual children and the class as a whole. And, when I combine this information with what I've learned from them through conferring and what they made, I get smarter about teaching and learning implications for individual children, small-group work, and whole-class minilessons.

My conferring work with children

The figure below shows the notes I took while listening in to children talking about nonfiction learning—I was noticing and then naming what they said. The quotation marks identify what children said; the parentheses identify my naming. These notes also help me identify future minilessons, and the children who inspire the lessons often help me teach them.

Finally, I bring together *small, needs-based groups* sparingly during the workshop—I'm convinced that one-on-one conferences serve children best. When I plan, I ask, "Are there children from today's workshop with like needs who would benefit from small-group work *more* than they would benefit from a conference?" If so, I bring them together out of efficiency. We meet anywhere from five to six minutes—I keep the meeting short and try to give them just enough information to keep going. If there are several children who are having difficulty during the workshop, I bring them together, too, to sort things out and then send them back out. Readers' workshop is all about growing proficient, independent, agentive readers. We all need to be mindful to not overscaffold children—it sends the message we don't believe they *can*. And so of course if we don't, they won't either.

My listening-in notes

That's the overview of all the pieces of workshop planning I wanted to pull together. Take note how I synthesized that information into a daily planning document for workshop (see right).

Everything about this shift in planning puts children front and center. And even though we might be confident that we've been putting children first all along, it's important to acknowledge the disequilibrium this shift creates, specifically around what happens when we get to planning for the minilesson. Why? Because our teaching might not be as authentic and student-centered as we think. When I think about myself, I wonder if there a was a bit of ego involved too—could it be that I thought my teaching was more important than children's doing?

Learning target:

_____

Worktime:

_____

_____

Mini lesson:

_____

Reflection:

_____

sequences for Teaching and Learning

Learning target:
What are we getting smarter about today? (What's our purpose?) And~ Why does this matter?

Worktime:
* What will children write, draw, or create that will give them (and us) concrete evidence of how they are approaching or meeting the target?
* What will they read?
* What will they talk about?

Mini lesson:
* What will children need from me to work with more depth and stamina than they would alone?

Reflection:
* How will children synthesize their learning for themselves and others?

What teaching and learning sequences will best meet childrens' needs today?

sequences for Teaching and Learning

Daily workshop planning

▨ Figuring Out What to Teach

First-grade teacher Emily Finney and I were having a conversation about retelling—it was part of an upcoming comprehension unit, and we wanted to look at this age-old skill in a fresh way. When asking children to retell, we expect them to make connections between what they already know about how stories work and apply it to the new stories they listen to and read. We want them to use their own words to retell what's important in a way that makes sense, without telling too much.

What could we do to help them get there? What authentic supports could we put into play that would engage children during work time and lead to student agency and independence? Emily and I weren't sure.

Whenever I'm stuck—whether it's about how to teach retelling, synthesizing information, nonfiction text structures, or something else—one of my go-to

strategies is to think about what I do as a reader first. How do I go about doing this? What helps me most? Sometimes we underestimate ourselves and jump online to see what other people say and do. But before doing that, give yourself fifteen or twenty minutes to dig in and think about how *you* go about it. It will be time well spent—you'll know more than you did before, and when you're aware of what you do (and you're learning from your kids about what they do), your understanding will continue to deepen.

> **Dear Reader,** You know more than you think you do. If you're not so sure about that, please know that all teachers feel this way now and again. Maybe this kind of thinking is new to you and you'll find yourself drawing a blank or feeling uncertain. But remember, you are a reader. You make meaning when you read. This is all about becoming **aware** of what you **already** do. You might want to get together with a colleague or two and think about what each of you do. You'll discover there's not one right, best way. Find **your** way. Learn from each other. Show kids how you go about it, and send them off to have a go. In time they'll find their own way, too; your lesson will be a springboard to new thinking. We want children to discover what works for them, just as you did.
> —Debbie

That's just what Emily and I did when we were thinking about how to teach retelling in a new way—we thought about what we do when we want to tell someone else what a book is about. When someone asks me about a book I've read, I can't always remember. But if I can call to mind a specific image from the book in question, it sparks my memory and I'm back in the game. It's the images—and sometimes one particular one—that help me remember what the story is about.

Emily and I wondered, "Could this same strategy work for children?" Could a single, memorable image lead to a retell? We didn't know for sure, but we were intrigued. We decided to give it a go and see what we could learn.

But first we needed to do some envisioning—what would meaningful work look like for these first graders? We began by envisioning the process—what would kids actually *do* to bring the learning target (*I can use mental images to help me retell and remember stories*) to life? We envisioned children seated in the meeting area, looking through stacks of books Emily had read aloud (or books from their book boxes), and talking together about the stories and their memorable images. We saw ourselves on the floor with them, listening in and talking with them.

We then tried to imagine what kids would make—what might they do (beyond talking) to make their thinking visible? We envisioned a big square in the middle of the paper: children could draw their most memorable image there, and in the space on either side of the square, they could write (or draw) what happened before and after.

We thought about authenticity—is this something readers do in the world? Almost. When I call to mind a specific image, I'm not actually drawing it and then writing what happened before and after. But that's what I'm doing in my head. We were making this process concrete for kids this first time around. If this was something that clicked with them, in time it would become something they'd do naturally, in their minds. This "make" was about making an invisible process visible.

Check out our draft of the thinking sheet and how we turned it into our final product!

Name _____
Title _____

I can use mental images to help me remember and retell stories.

What happened before?

My Memorable Image

What happened after?

Sticky notes—
images
words
both

Day 2 - Big Idea? Attach to bottom of this page—Maybe a big sticky note?

Our brainstorming for the thinking sheet

My name is _____
The title of my book is_____

I can use mental images to help me retell and remember stories.

My Memorable Image

The thinking sheet

What do you notice about children's work? I wonder if they would remember what their stories were about a year later?

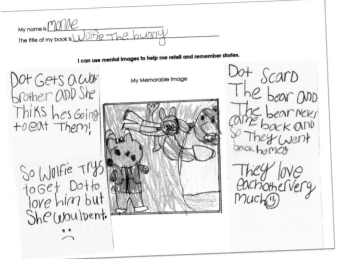

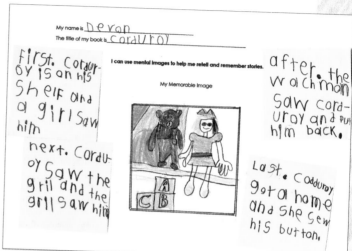

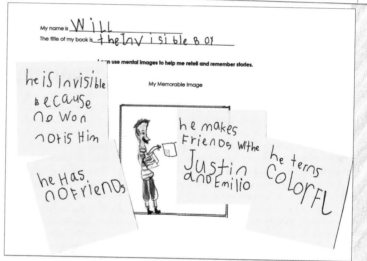

Mental images

Emily knew that creating images isn't the only way to retell, but it's a way in—a way to begin the conversation about how and why this is something that readers do. In the days ahead, she'd be conferring, observing, listening in to student conversations, and paying attention to the processes they'd be using. She was open to possibilities, knowing she'd learn from them and they'd learn from each other as they found their own paths. She'd be nurturing a community of discovery, independence, and the collective sense of agency.

As children discover and adopt new strategies, they can become teachers of minilessons or small groups, too—think about the messages this sends!

There's no need for us to feel this huge pressure about exactly how to teach children something new. We show kids one way, and they try it out, reflect, and discover new ways too. Children need to try lots of ways to figure out what works best for them. The message is we're all learners in this classroom. And yes, we're all teachers, too!

Teaching children to think about retelling in this way differs from common packaged lesson plans, where there is just one right way (and therefore lots of wrong ways) to do things. This is problematic for children and teachers—it restricts innovation and creativity and offers nothing for children who might process things in another way in order to be successful. Don't we want to present possibilities to children and invite them to try things out to see what works best for them? If we believe in student agency, our answer has to be yes. And I suspect Will, Natalie, Monae, Devon, and the rest of the kids in Emily Finney's class would agree.

▓ Playing with the Sequence

When I worked with Emily on planning for a workshop on retelling, Emily and I thought through *what* children would read, write, and talk about first. What came next was thinking about *when* she would teach and when children would have work time.

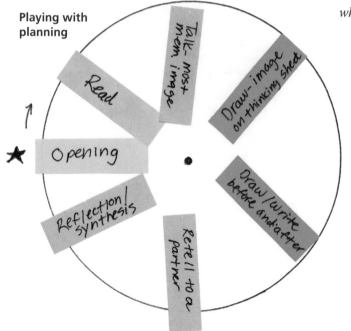

Playing with planning

This particular workshop had a lot of moving pieces. To help us plan, we color-coded sticky notes and manipulated them until we figured out the best sequence for children to read, write, and talk, doing our best to ensure authenticity and balance. You probably wouldn't use the sticky notes this way to plan every day, but it's one way to think things through when figuring out what work time will look like.

❖ *Read.*

❖ Identify their most memorable image from the book they are reading and *talk* about it with a partner.

❖ *Draw* their image in the square on their thinking sheet.

❖ *Write* or *draw* what came before and after their memorable image.

❖ *Talk*—retell their story to a partner.

Only then did we plan the minilesson! We asked ourselves two things:

❖ How can we best help children work with more agency than they would without any instruction at all?

❖ Where in the read, write, and talk sequences will they need our instruction and support most?

Emily and I placed the minilesson after drawing their memorable image and before writing or drawing (retelling) what came before and after their image. We believed this is where children would need the most explicit instruction and support.

"What?" you might be thinking. "The minilesson doesn't have to come first?" If so, you're not alone—those words were once my words too. I used to think the workshop sequence—the minilesson, independent reading, and the share—was fixed. But now I understand that the workshop, just like the gradual release of responsibility instructional model, doesn't have to be as linear as I once thought. Now

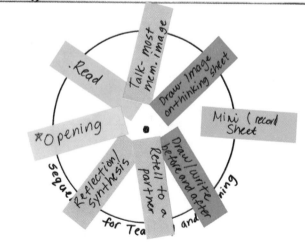

Final Plan

I'm thinking that workshops (as well as other structures) can offer teachers a reflective, *dynamic* process for planning that allows for teachers to be flexible and make key instructional decisions about what will best serve children on any given day.

Much of my work focuses on long- and short-term planning with teachers, in a variety of settings and structures. When we get to the day-to-day planning, and I propose we temporarily reconfigure the structure that's in place to better meet the needs of children, they sometimes look at me in disbelief.

"Is this allowed?" they ask. Or, "Can I really do that?"

Of course you can!

Structures are essential—they guide us as we plan, and they serve children and teachers well most of the time. But on the days they don't, we have the power and the responsibility to adapt them as children's needs warrant it.

What the Research Tells Us

In the coda of "Comprehension Going Forward," David Pearson (2011) speaks to the gradual release of responsibility instructional model. He writes: "But it does not mean, as many infer, that we always begin a sequence with modeling, then moving to guided practice, and finally moving to independent practice. We could begin a sequence by asking students to 'try it on their own,' offering feedback and assistance as students demonstrate the need for it." (248)

As teachers practice, learn, and grow, the structures we use for teaching and learning evolve right along with us. It's not that I'm about reinventing workshop, but I am about flexibility, adaptation, and thinking about workshop (or any structure) in new ways that serve children and put their needs first. I understand now that the workshop structure isn't something we do by heart. Workshops are something we do *with* heart.

Following are some other ways I've adapted workshop sequences.

Have you ever thought it might make sense to start the workshop with independent reading instead of a minilesson? What about starting with work time or even a share? All of these are possible in a readers' workshop. For example, say you're diving into a new unit, and you believe it's vital to engage children in the whole of the topic first, before you jump in with a set of specific lessons and tasks. Could you simply pose a guiding question and send children off to see what they could figure out?

You could!

And at the same time children would be in discovery mode, you would be too. You'd be sitting alongside them, listening in, asking questions, taking notes, learning about where children were, and thinking about what they would need from you and each other to learn and grow in the days and weeks to come.

Or maybe you're near the end of a study, and you know that, more than anything else, children need time to read and write, and you need time to confer with them individually about their end-of-unit demonstrations of understanding. Is it OK to skip the minilesson in favor of teaching and learning with children one-on-one?

It is.

Remember, just because you don't have a minilesson, it doesn't mean you're not teaching—our most effective teaching occurs when we confer with children one-on-one (Allington). On this particular day, a whole-class lesson wouldn't benefit the majority of children, so why have one? Having more time to learn, differentiate, and plan with individual children makes the most sense.

This is how structures are supposed to work! They're designed to accommodate and facilitate teaching and learning, not stifle, control, or interfere with them.

When we put children first, planning isn't as hard as you might think. Regardless of the structures we use, we need only ask ourselves two compelling questions:

1. What do children need most today?

2. How will my structure for teaching and learning support their needs?

Let's take a look first at the classic structure of the workshop and then shift to a variety of ways we might adapt it to better meet the needs of the children in front of us.

Here's the key for the classic graphic (see figures) and the six workshop sequences that follow:

▨ *Opening*

▨ *Student and teacher work time*

▨ *Minilesson*

▨ *Reflection and teaching share*

The Classic

The classic structure of a readers' workshop gives children time to learn during a minilesson; read, write, talk, and confer with their teacher during work time; and teach and learn from each other during reflection and sharing.

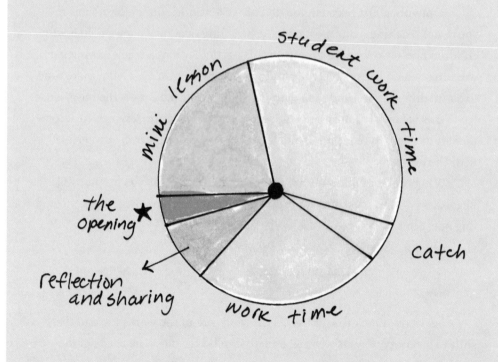

The Liftoff

Any time I'm launching a new unit, whether it's a genre study, an author study, a content study, or something else, I believe what children need most—across the grades—is immersion in the topic first, before I jump in with a list of learning targets and minilessons. Giving children time to explore the whole of a topic— getting a feel for the big picture instead of breaking it down into parts right away—builds and broadens background knowledge; increases student engagement, curiosity, discovery, and agency; and paves the way for understanding.

What's the role of the teacher during liftoff? Teachers are actively kid-

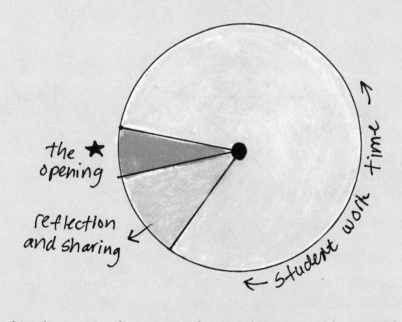

watching: listening in, observing, conferring, taking notes, and more. We're learning valuable information about children's understandings, their misconceptions, what they need to grow, and how to design our upcoming lessons (and workshop sequences) with specificity and confidence.

The Have-a-Go

Peter Johnston (2004) describes the "thrill" of children figuring out something for themselves. We want to give children plenty of opportunities to realize that they are the kind of people who can discover things on their own. The have-a-go workshop is perfect for this kind of discovery.

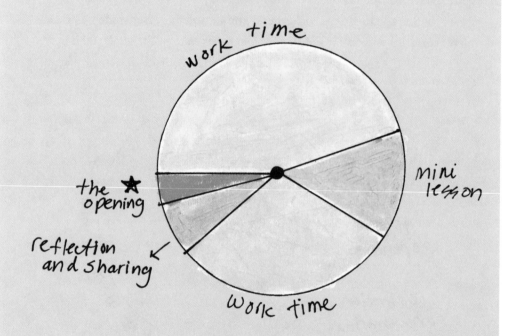

Or, maybe you're not quite sure what children need. Have individual and table-talk conferences (where you talk with small groups of children at their tables or wherever they are) to get a better sense of where children are. Once you have some insights, bring everyone back together. Use the minilesson to share what you've learned, listen to children, and send them back out with some new things to think about and try.

The Let-Them-Read

Maybe you've just finished a big study, and kids need some time to, well, *breathe*. Children choose what they want to read. You get to confer with them and learn. Maybe it's for one day or maybe it's for five. But, oh my goodness, pure perfection!

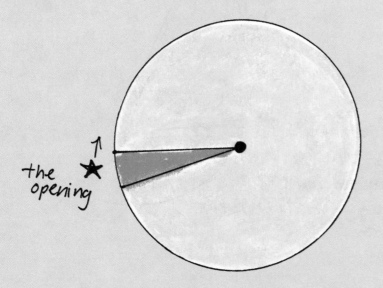

the ★ opening

Or maybe there's an assembly right in the middle of reading time, or it's a half-day, or it's the day before winter break, or it's a late-start day because of snow or rain or ice. No worries. Give them a gift. Let them read.

Or just maybe your lessons have been running long the past day or two. Make it up to them. Just let them, you know, read.

The Skinny

Maybe most children are on their way to meeting their goals for the current unit and all they really need is time to keep going, confer with you, and talk with each other.

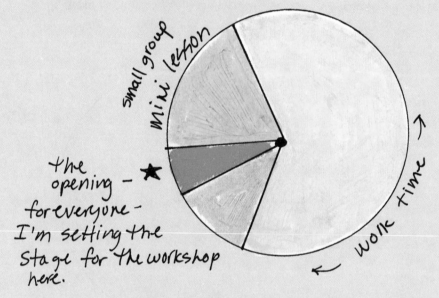

And maybe there are four or five children who need more support from you. Why gather the whole group for a lesson today if only a few need you? Similar in structure to the classic, the minilesson in the skinny is tailored to meet the needs of a small group of children with similar needs, rather than the whole class. Following the lesson, I spend my time conferring with others and perhaps checking in with the children in the small group to see how they're applying what we've just talked about.

Most often, small, needs-based group work occurs during the work time. But on occasion, when a whole-class minilesson isn't necessary for everyone, the skinny fills the bill. And sometimes, when the whole class is working in small, inquiry- or interest-based groups, it might make sense to meet with each group during the workshop, listening in, asking questions, encouraging children to talk about what, if anything, is tripping them up, and sharing what you've noticed. Then support them as needed.

The Double-Time

Because children's books need to be worthy of what we're asking them to do, their choices are out of necessity guided so they can be successful. But children need free-choice reading, too. If there isn't time outside the workshop, put it inside! The example below shows free-choice reading in the beginning of the workshop, but it could also be near the end, right after the share.

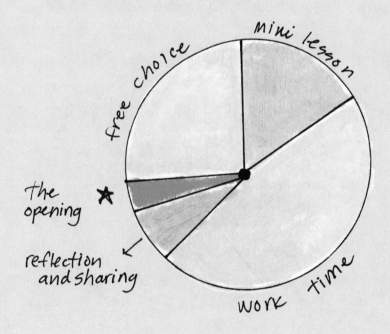

The Shift-the-Share

Sometimes it feels right to put the reflection and share time right up front. Maybe children need to think through and share where they are going today and how they're planning to get there. They take a few quiet moments to plan, think through (in their heads or in their notebooks), and set themselves up for work time. As children share their plans they may discover others are working on the same thing and decide to work together, or they may have suggestions or recommendations.

  Or maybe work time went long the day before, and there wasn't time to share. No worries! You can begin with the share. Then you could move to a minilesson or go straight from the share to work time, depending on what feels right. And really, you could even place the share in the middle of work time—coming together and getting inspiration from others might be just the thing children need most.

> "How we spend our days is, of course,
> how we spend our lives."
> —ANNIE DILLARD, *THE WRITING LIFE*

▨ Taking Ownership

When I adapt the key elements of a workshop (minilesson, work time, and the reflection and share), I work to stay true to its guiding principles (time, choice, response, and community) and my beliefs about teaching and learning. I ask myself the following questions:

✤ *Purpose*: What's my purpose for reconfiguring the workshop? How will it benefit children's social and learning needs? And, if asked, could I explain the *why* of my lesson in a clear, knowledgeable, and confident way?

✤ *Time*: Will children be reading, writing, and talking for at least two-thirds of the workshop?

✤ *Choice*: Are the books children will read worthy of what I am asking them to do? Will there be a balance between free and guided choice throughout the school day, in the workshop, or both?

✤ *Conferring*: Which kids need me most today, and what do they need? Am I ready?

✤ *Response*: Do readers in the world do the kinds of reading work that I'm asking children to do? Is the focus on making meaning and understanding? Does it give children and me the information we need to figure out where they are and set goals for where they need to go next?

✤ *Talk*: Are there opportunities during the workshop for children to talk together about their books, how they're applying what I'm working to teach them, and what they're learning about reading and themselves as readers?

✤ *Community*: Is the spirit one of collaboration rather than competition? Is there the collective sense of agency—a "we are the kind of kids who can figure things out together" kind of feel?

Taking ownership of our teaching and children's learning changes everything. We own it when things go well, and we own it when they don't. But please know that no matter what you do, or how much time you spend, all workshops won't go as planned *or* envisioned. It's our reaction to lessons gone awry that matters most. Sometimes, when things fall apart, we choose the easy way out and hold children responsible for what went wrong. In our darkest moments, we may even say things like, "These kids just aren't ready for something like this," or "My class this year is so low," or "I just need to stick to the basics with these kids—they can't handle choice, or talking together during work time, or really anything except sitting in their seats."

But what if, instead, we owned the whole mess? What if we switched our thinking from finding fault with children to asking, "What can *I* learn from this? What do children need from me tomorrow to be successful? How can I scaffold them *just enough* so that they can get started and move forward? What can I do and not do, and say and not say, that will let children know I believe in them?"

In other words: Own it. Think about what kids need most. Trust yourself and move forward.

Some days we make the right calls; other days we don't. But we don't sit down and cry. Well, maybe for a minute or two, but we come right back, stronger than before, remembering and believing that we have what it takes to figure things out for tomorrow. This is the constant challenge, isn't it? How can I best teach kids tomorrow based on what I learned from them today? *And* what did I learn about myself as a teacher today that will help me be a better teacher in the days and weeks to come?

And really, all that a "bad" lesson shows us is that there is some piece of information we are missing. We change things by using work time to discover what we need to know about our children and our teaching, just as our students are using it to discover things about themselves as readers and learners—this is how we keep moving forward, growing our practice and growing readers.

And here's another thing: don't some of our best lessons follow on the heels of a particularly dreary one? So see? We may even *need* some not-so-great lessons to move us forward—they stop us in our tracks, cause us to reflect, rethink, reenergize, and reenvision, and help us work again to be our very best selves.

It needs to be said that allowing people to make decisions about what happens to them is inherently preferable to controlling them. It is more respectful and consistent with basic values to which most of us claim to subscribe. Apart from the skills that will be useful for students to have in the future, they ought to have a chance to choose in the present. Children, after all, are not just adults-in-the-making. They are people whose current needs and rights and experiences must be taken seriously. Put it this way: students should not only be trained to live in a democracy when they grow up; they should have the chance to live in one today.

—ALFIE KOHN

"CHOICES FOR CHILDREN: WHY AND HOW TO LET STUDENTS DECIDE" (1993)

CHAPTER 3

What If Our Classroom Environment and Routines Offered Choice?

Control leads to compliance, autonomy leads to engagement.

—DANIEL PINK, *DRIVE* (2011, 108)

 **Finding Our Way to a Beautiful Question: Frustration over Supplies**

Time can go quickly in the classroom. There's the rapid progression that happens because we're in flow, joyfully engaged in the meaningful learning of that moment. And then, there's the other kind: staccato time, the time we lose to unnecessary interruptions. Tanya needs a pencil, James can't find his reading folder, and Leah had some sticky notes but now they're gone. We give Tanya a pencil, find James' folder hiding in the depths of his backpack, and peel off a few sticky notes for Leah. Whew. But now Steven needs to go to the bathroom and there's no pass, and so does Ramon, and Madison is in Daniel's reading spot, and he's about to cry. Oh my.

What the Research Tells Us

* Researchers Hilda Borko and Richard Shavelson summarized studies that reported [we make an average of up to] .7 decisions per minute during interactive teaching.
* Researcher Philip Jackson (Cuban, 149) said that elementary teachers have 200 to 300 exchanges with students every hour (between 1200–1500 a day), most of which are unplanned and unpredictable, calling for teacher decisions, if not judgments. (Cuban 2011)

All of this in-the-moment decision making would be enough to push most people over the edge, but teachers handle it. We choose to bring resolution to these issues quickly, but maybe we're doing children (and ourselves) a disservice by fixing problems for them.

Routines can help minimize these interruptions: we can teach children how to problem solve some of the things that interrupt their work and our teaching time. But can routines do more than minimize interruptions? Might they also help teach children how to have greater agency, choice, and independence? I'd been working with a group of teachers to think about student and teacher agency throughout the day, particularly during student work time. We'd read and discussed Peter Johnston's *Choice Words* (2004) and the specific challenges to their practice. On this morning, teachers talked together in small groups and recorded their thinking about ownership and agency on a whiteboard:

Our Thinking About Ownership and Agency

What are we doing for children that they could be doing for themselves?

Choice is essential for student and teacher ownership and agency.

I'm the kind of kid / I'm the kind of teacher who can figure things out.

"The teacher must view the present child as capable, and on that basis imagine new possibilities." (Johnston 2004)

The ones doing the work are the ones getting smarter.

"We need to look at the kinds of stories we arrange for children to tell themselves." (Johnston 2004, 30)

"Believing, 'Yes, I imagine I can do this' is as important for children as it is for teachers." (Johnston 2004, 29)

It's all about teachers trusting children, children trusting teachers, and teachers trusting themselves.

Our thinking about ownership and agency

All this conversation had been focused on developing children's ownership and agency as readers specifically, but after lunch Adam asked, "I know this isn't exactly related to what's up next, but could we please take a minute to talk about the pencils? I never seem to have enough and I'm spending way too much time and energy trying to manage this one little thing. Does anyone else have this problem?"

Teachers smiled. Some nodded. Two clapped. And then the floodgates opened. Another teacher voiced frustration with sticky notes: "My kids always want more, and I can't keep up." And so it went, one supply after another. It was clear we needed to follow this conversation through because helping children access and manage basic supplies was taking precious time away from teaching reading.

It was then our conversation shifted to thinking more deeply about the routines they used for managing basic supplies. As teachers shared in small groups, they realized that many of these were teacher-directed, overly complicated, and time-consuming. Children came to them for supplies because they'd established that expectation. They worked to understand why they felt the need to control so many things—pencils, markers, staplers, paper, and sticky notes, as well as what children read, where they read, and the partners they read and talked with.

The more they talked, the more they wondered if their need to control things was rooted in fear, insecurity, and a lack of trust and confidence in what children might do if they didn't.

And then came these zingers:

❖ Does all this managing of supplies take time away from the most important things we could be spending time on—things like conferring with children, listening in to their conversations, and making notes to help us plan for tomorrow?

❖ Could this possibly be about us wanting to feel or be needed?

❖ Could our issues around control be sabotaging student agency and independence?

❖ And finally, when we say, "Our kids aren't ready for this kind of independence," are we really saying, "*We* aren't ready"?

Now we knew for sure that these were all *big* little things and worthy of our time. (Thanks, Adam!)

What's the Best That Could Happen? Managing Their Own Work

Managing supplies seems like such a small thing. It's something we might not think that much about, but by asking a simple question, Adam showed us that there's no action during learning time that's insignificant: everything contributes to or hinders children's learning. This challenges us to look closely at the seemingly mundane details of our practice in order to consider how our use of time supports our goals of nurturing children's ownership and agency. When we talk about teaching, we always talk about time: how much time should we spend on a minilesson, a conference, a read-aloud, a unit? The answer is always based on what the children in our classrooms need.

I have yet to meet a student who doesn't need to learn more about how to manage his or her own work. Honestly, we're all—every adult I know included—works in progress on this topic: sometimes we're focused and efficient; sometimes, not so much. When a supply—my phone—stopped working, I was a mess. I wasted so much time trying to figure it out before I finally decided to head over to the Apple store and have them fix it for me. That period of flailing about was demoralizing; I felt much less capable than I usually do . . . and I, like you, have had years of experience of competency in a variety of areas! When students don't know what to do when they don't have the supply they need, or feel that they're not permitted to get what they need, they don't just feel less competent as pencil getters—they feel less competent as human beings. And when we are under attack by interruptions, our patience, attention, and ability to think deeply are under attack, too.

What the Research Tells Us

"The distraction of an interruption, combined with the brain drain of preparing for that interruption, made our test takers 20 percent dumber." (Sullivan and Thompson 2013)

When measuring "various dimensions of stress, . . . people scored significantly higher when interrupted. They had higher levels of stress, frustration, mental effort, feeling of time pressure and mental workload." (Mark 2008)

Whole-class art piece inspired by Van Gogh

Photo by Barb Smith

That's why routines and a thoughtfully planned classroom environment are essential to children's learning and our teaching. We problem solve as much as we can before difficulties arise so that we can minimize them. Because learning and teaching *are* difficult, we don't need to add to that burden unnecessarily. And yet we don't want to create an environment that presents such narrowly constricted choices that children really don't have any choice at all. We don't want to eliminate difficulty; we want to offer authentic possibilities for children to navigate it, so that they're holding onto their personal agency and independence. This can sound subtle until we consider what the specifics of routines and classroom environments can look like.

Choice within routines and environment is essential for instilling agency. Without choice, children are blindly following our rules and expectations. We might get interrupted less frequently, but they're thinking less frequently and still overrelying on our direction, which is never our goal. Early-in-the-year conversations with children about routines and environment help invite them to think for themselves, take specific action to solve their own problems, and help each other do this too. They also allow us to show children who we are, what we're about, and what we believe about who they are and what they can do. We're sending messages from the get-go: *We're in this together. I trust you. I believe in your capacity to make smart decisions, and I'll support you every way I can.* When we start with the most basic understandings about how they navigate their learning through routines and environment, we set up a foundation for how they will navigate all of their learning experiences within and beyond our classroom.

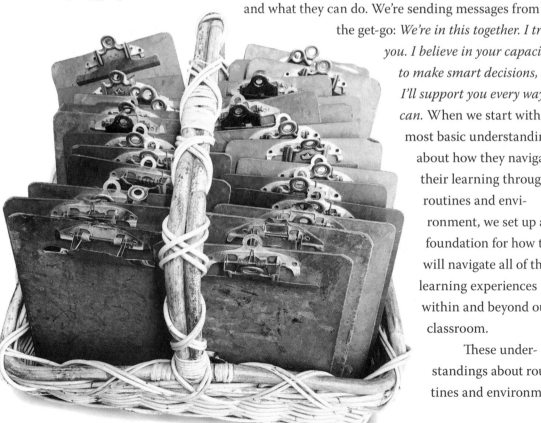

These understandings about routines and environment

Photo by Barb Smith

aren't just about supporting children's growth but about reminding ourselves of what we, as teachers, should and shouldn't control. For me the answer is simple—there's no need for us to do anything for children that they can do for themselves. It's a simple answer, but sometimes we default to controlling things because it just seems easier than thinking through what's best for children's growth. While it may be easier in the moment—to find another pencil for Tanya—those moments add up to make our teaching and children's learning more difficult. Every unnecessary interruption tears at the concentration we need to teach. It's not just the moment of the interruption but the time we need to refocus after we've been interrupted. That accumulates into less time to talk with children about the real work of readers and to observe them reading. Likewise, children become distracted from doing that work by not knowing how to navigate the obstacles of getting to it. We need to shift from distracted teachers and students to focused teachers and students. Focused as in *self-regulated*—not controlled or compliant, but in control of themselves. That means we don't dominate the beginning of the year with predetermined rules about what children must do to please their teacher, but instead make the beginning of the year about teachers and children coming together to figure out how to make their classroom community a place that will serve everyone well.

When we create situations where children are empowered, we're empowered, too. When accessible and authentic environments and routines are in place, we're no longer rushing around in fix-it mode; we're able to focus our energy on what matters most and free ourselves up to do the work we need and want to do—teach, learn, and imagine real possibilities for children and ourselves.

And think about this: If we help children realize that they can find their way out of difficulty with supplies, imagine what they can do beyond that. Just maybe they'll see themselves as the kind of people who can figure their way out of difficulty well enough to help other people find their way.

▒▒ Being Intentional in Our Language

I've been a teacher for what seems like forever, and when I think back to my days in the classroom, these are the things I remember saying over and over and over again:

❖ "Remember what you can do?"

❖ "You knew what to do all along, didn't you? I *knew* you were the kind of kid who . . ."

❖ "I trust you to do the right thing."

Sometimes it's hard for kids to believe they're allowed to make decisions like these, but this kind of language assures them not only that they can, but also that we expect them to! It helps them hold onto their freedom—it reinforces and supports them as they learn to assume more and more responsibility for their actions and their learning. We're helping children internalize that we trust and believe in them. This kind of language arranges the kinds of stories we're hoping they'll tell about themselves. In time, our language becomes their language, which leads to this kind of agentive, proactive talk: "Oh, wait! I know just what to do! I can . . ."

Here are some examples of teacher language that reinforces children's agency and ownership:

❖ "Your red marker isn't working anymore? Remember what you can do? Throw it away, go to the drawer that holds our markers, and take a brand-new red one. You don't have to ask or tell me, remember? I trust you to do the right thing."

❖ "You want to sit in the red chair, but Fin is already there, right? So what could you do now? Ah—find another spot? You knew what to do all along, didn't you?"

❖ "You need more sticky notes? No worries. Remember what you can do? That's right—just get some more out of the drawer, and put them in the basket at your table. Next time, you don't even have to ask! I trust you to do the right thing."

❖ "You forgot to bring your book back from home? It's OK. Bring it back tomorrow and then you can take another one."

❖ "Your pencil needs sharpening? No worries. Remember how we decided to fix this problem? Put your pencil in the 'Sharpen Me' can, and take one from the 'I'm Sharp' can. You don't have to ask or tell me, remember? I trust you to do the right thing."

❖ "You need to go to the bathroom? Remember? You don't have to ask me. Take a look at the clipboard hanging by the door. Take a pass, write your name on the next line, and off you go. You know I trust you to do the right thing."

❖ "You need a pencil and some sticky notes at home? I'm so glad
you told me. Stay a minute after school today and I'll help you
get all set up."

Our language sets children up for being the kind of people who make
and take responsibility for their own choices and who believe that other people
should have the freedom to make their own choices too. Yes, routines scaffold
children's decision making, but it all begins with the beliefs we hold, what we
say, and how we say it.

The truth is that, if we want children to take responsibility for their own
behavior, we must first *give* them responsibility, and plenty of it.

In Emily Callahan's fourth-grade classroom, children take responsibility
for their behavior all day long, but it's the first thirty minutes of the day these
fourth graders love most. It's choice time, and they make decisions about what
they want to do, how and where they'll do it, and if they'll work independently or
with others. They have full access to their classroom and school libraries, digital
devices, and supplies. They might decide to delve into a topic that interests them,
teach friends something they've learned, work on a project of choice, create a
club, and of course do some free-choice reading or writing. Their classroom
environment supports their work, allowing them space (literally and figura-
tively!) to make decisions, learn about themselves and each other, and grow their
sense of agency, day after day after day. (Which of course is what it takes!)

Emily explicitly teaches during reading and writing workshops, but throughout this early-morning time she's mostly observing children, listening in, and learning about kids, their choices, and how they're expressing their developing sense of agency.

Let me introduce you to two groups of children I conferred with one day during this time—I'll call them the Poetry Boys and the

Poetry

There are
no rules,
no barriers
no limits.

No words
can define
Poetry
but Poetry
defines
the words,
You
can set it up how ever you want,

Poetry is
words through
passed
the heart,

"The Poetry Boys"

Boys' poetry club

Book-Club Girls. First, meet Maverick, Robbie, and Aiden.

Surrounded by stacks of poetry books, their notebooks, markers, pencils, and some of the poems they'd written over the year (one framed), these boys were sprawled on the floor, collaborating on their latest poem.

I joined them and asked about their poetry club and how it worked.

"You've gotta read the poem about the Royals first!" Robbie said, handing me a baseball-themed picture frame with a poem inside: "World Series (We Hope)." "It might not be our best poem, but it's our most exciting one."

Robbie was right—it was pretty exciting! I congratulated them all on their eventual World Series win, and we moved to thinking about their poetry club. "Well, first of all, it's like we are a little family," Robbie said. "And we all do different things."

"Yeah," Maverick said. "We didn't even know each other that well until the poetry club, and now we know what's inside each other's hearts. We're really good friends now."

Aiden wondered if they should write all this down for me, and of course I said yes, please! (Get ready. I think you're about to fall in love with these three young poets too!)

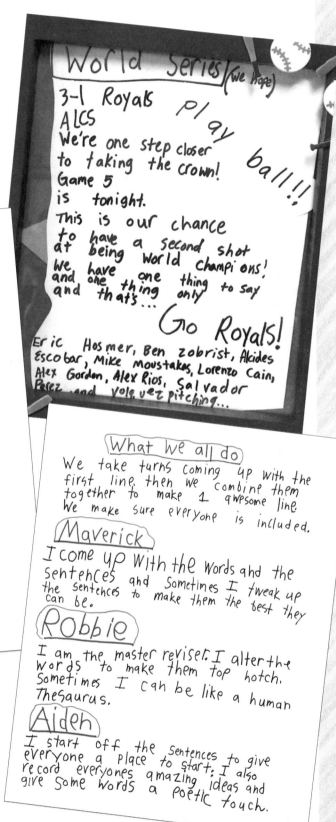

The poetry club

We are
a small family
brought together
by 3
small poet's hearts.

Poetry has made
our friendship
stronger.
Our goal
is to inspire.

Our poetry club
has strengthened
our love
of poetry
at an amazing
rate.

World Series (we hope)
3-1 Royals
ALCS
We're one step closer
to taking the crown!
Game 5
is tonight.
This is our chance
to have a second shot
at being World Champions!
We have one thing
and one thing only to say
and that's...
Go Royals!

Eric Hosmer, Ben Zobrist, Alcides
Escobar, Mike Moustakas, Lorenzo Cain,
Alex Gordon, Alex Rios, Salvador
Perez, and Volquez pitching...

What we all do
We take turns coming up with the
first line. then we combine them
together to make 1 awesome line.
We make sure everyone is included.

Maverick
I come up with the words and the
sentences and sometimes I tweak up
the sentences to make them the best they
can be.

Robbie
I am the master reviser. I alter the
words to make them top hotch.
Sometimes I can be like a human
Thesaurus.

Aiden
I start off the sentences to give
everyone a place to start. I also
record everyones amazing ideas and
give some words a poetic touch.

Here's what they wrote:

Aiden, Robbie, and Maverick came together because they wanted to learn more about poetry, and they left learning much more than that. They made their own decisions about how things were going to work, and mostly they

The time had come: Aiden, Maverick, and Robbie gave their final poem of the year to their teacher, Emily.

read poetry, wrote poetry, and talked poetry, defining it for themselves. Any one of us might have jumped in and started teaching them about meter, or rhyme, or different types of poems, but Emily resisted—she knew there was plenty of time for that. She saw how they were thinking about their work and knew that if she gave them space to explore while holding themselves responsible to each other, they'd do great things.

Now let's meet the Book-Club Girls. Faith, Bayleigh, and Tanyia were also in Emily's class, and I met with them next. They, too, were hard at work, thinking about how to organize a book club. I observed and listened in as Faith pulled out a pile of papers from her notebook. "So I typed up our rules and stuff last night," she said, spreading out copies.

Remember, five minutes ago I was with the Poetry Boys, and now I was thinking, "Wait a minute. Did I really just read these words, and in all caps?" DON'T COME TO THE MEETINGS IF YOU HAVE NOTHING TO SAY TO US, No SLACKING ON READING, NO BLURTING, and (my favorite) DON'T STRESS OUT. (It might be hard not to!) Yikes, where did all this come from?

Name _____ rules! _____
number:#

1.No SLACKING ON READING
2. TELL US IF YOU ARE BORED ON THE BOOK SO WE CAN ASSIGN YOU A NEW ONE.
3. DON'T COME TO THE MEETINGS IF YOU HAVE NOTHING TO SAY TO US.
4. DO READ your assigned book or tell us you don't like it.
5. DO LISTEN TO THE PERSON TALKING
6. BE RESPECTFUL
7. READ 2 CHAPTERS A DAY.
8. no ignoring people.
9.don't stress out.
10. no blurting.

---

meeting days

monday: read in the group silent for 20-25 minutes then we will talk about the chapter.
tuesday: talking about our characters in the books.
wednesday: read to self.
thursday: we will talk about character actions and feelings.
Friday: meeting about the main lesson.
these are the meeting days or the days you will read a chapter just 2 a day thought don't read more than that.
don't miss a meeting or slacking off on reading chapters.

saturday: read 1 chapter
sunday: read 1 chapter

Book-Club Girls' rules

name pleas[e]
readers log

1. _____
2. _____
3. _____
4. _____
5. _____
6. _____
7. _____
8. _____
9. _____
10. _____
11. please tell TANYIA + FAITH + BAILEY about each chapter on this log.
12. please only read 2 chapters a day.
13. _____
14. _____
15. _____

Sign up sheet!

NAME:

NO SLACKING!

do you agree to listen to TANYIA + FAITH + BAYLEIGHY and to participate in the work we're doing and to treat supplies nicely!
please state name;
signature;
do you promise to do all of above; yes or NO! circle.

The reality is that all of us can default to being controlling under certain conditions. We consciously strive to use language that is invitational and noncontrolling, not just for the children we're teaching but for ourselves.. We think before we speak: Does what I'm about to say imply control and/or expect compliance? (If it does, we change it!) Emily had been very thoughtful about promoting agency in her classroom and offered her children plenty of positive, specific language, but these girls had already internalized language from other experiences. This isn't about judging the girls or the teaching that might have led them to such controlling ideas. The work we need to do when we see this in our classroom is to figure out why children default to this kind of thinking when placed in a position of power. It's as if the girls were thinking: "This book club is ours. We own it. We get to make the rules." Could implementing rigid measures be children's default when they feel uncertain about how to proceed or how to share responsibility?

And could this be true for us, too?

Poetry Club

Invitational, Social, Fun

We make sure everyone is included.
No rules, no barriers, no limits.

Celebratory

We have made excellence, beauty.
Poetry is words passed through the heart.

Collaborative

We take turns.
Our goal is to inspire.
We . . . grew alongside others.

"Us," Reflective: See Strengths in Themselves and Others

Our poetry club has strengthened our love of poetry.
We are a small family brought together by three small poet's hearts.
Poetry has made our friendship stronger.

Book Club

Authoritative, Exclusive

Do you agree to listen?

Tedious, Task-Oriented

Please tell [us] about each chapter on this log.
Don't miss a meeting.

Controlling

No blurting.
Please only read two chapters a day.
Tell us if you are bored on the book so we can assign you a new one.

"We/They": See Strengths in Themselves; Assume Weakness in Others

Don't . . . slack off on reading chapters.
Don't come to the meetings if you have nothing to say to us.

Comparing stance and language between the Poetry Boys and the Book-Club Girls

Let's compare the stance and language of the two groups and see what we notice.

The Poetry Boys and Book-Club Girls reflected two different kinds of thinking about the world: "What's the best that could happen?" and "What's the worst that could happen?" When we envision the best that could happen, we're thinking of possibilities—we're open to new thinking, new ideas, new learning. When we envision the worst that could happen, we become fearful; we worry about what might go wrong. So we overscaffold, just to be safe. We restrict and limit new thinking, ideas, and learning, and the thrill of the figuring.

When Emily and I conferred with the Book-Club Girls later in the day, the girls were disappointed no one had signed up, and they wondered if it was the book—should they change it? Emily wondered aloud if the other book-club members might want to be part of the decision making—"It's their book club, too, right?" The girls decided to offer three choices, and they went from there.

This kind of work with children is a low-risk, high-reward proposition. Emily and I talked with the Book-Club Girls about all those rules and how they thought their words might make others feel. Then, as they realized that their language wasn't doing what they wanted, we invited them to consider new words by asking them what they thought Mrs. Callahan might say if she were starting a book club. That helped because Emily was working so thoughtfully to offer her children that kind of communication on a daily basis. It takes time for children to shift from an authoritarian point of view to a more democratic one. That's why this routine work isn't trivial. Imagining new possibilities—ones that contradict our past experience—isn't easy for any of us, and truly for most of us the only way we can do that is by having some glimpse of it through other people, having to transfer that model to specific situations, and getting feedback on how well it's working, just as the Book-Club Girls did.

▓ Cocreating Routines

When the Book-Club Girls had the opportunity to create their own routines, they learned some things about themselves and were able to shift toward being closer to who they wanted to be (plus their book club was better in every way). If Emily had given the Book-Club Girls a routine for their work, even an agentive one, they might not have grappled with some of their tendencies to control and limit their experience. This is why the scaffolding we provide should always be in setting up routines *with* students, rather than *for* them. We listen to their ideas for routines for accessing supplies over a week or two. We share our ideas, too, always going back to thinking about what people do in the world when they need things. This is about having a conversation, trying a routine out, thinking together about how we feel it's working, and making changes if we need too.

Scaffolding is like everything else—we do our best not to help children too much or too little, giving them just the right amount. We keep it simple. The more steps, the more rules, and the more things children need to worry about, the higher the chances are we're overscaffolding. Keep it simple and authentic.

Now let's take a look at the processes teachers and I used to rethink basic routines for managing pencils, sticky notes, and where children would work during independent reading time.

Process for Rethinking Routines

- ❖ Acknowledge the problem.
- ❖ Ask, "What concerns do I have?"
- ❖ Let go: Create an action-oriented, positively worded question.
- ❖ Evaluate solutions with the question, "Do these solutions advance student agency?"

What follows are some possibilities for thinking through routines; you'll want to consider what makes sense for you and the children in your class.

Pencils

All of us agreed: readers and writers, mathematicians and scientists, musicians and artists all need pencils. What do they all do when they need one? They get one! That's the way of the world. Could a simple "need one, get one" policy solve a complicated and time-consuming problem?

But how would that work? They'd just go get one—that's it? We talked about how we would discuss this with children in ways that would help them manage pencils on their own. We decided that a class meeting would allow the teacher and students to cocreate new routines that would empower children to take responsibility and ownership for the pencils.

To create authentic, student-centered routines for managing pencils, teachers came up with these questions:

❖ Where will we put our pencils so everyone can get one when they need one?

❖ How will we take care of them?

❖ What will happen if a pencil breaks or needs sharpening?

❖ When will we sharpen them?

❖ Who will do it?

Acknowledge the Problem.	Ask, "What Concerns Do We Have?"	Let Go: Create an Action-Oriented, Positively Worded Question.
Routines for managing pencils are complicated and time-consuming. Students get one pencil for the day. They check it out in the morning and check it in at the end of the day. If a pencil is misplaced, students need to try to find another one, borrow one, or buy one from their teacher or the office.	How many pencils do children really need? How can we motivate students to take care of them? (And not chew off the erasers?) How can we manage the never-ending din of the pencil sharpener?	How can we cocreate authentic, student-centered routines for managing our pencils?

Depending on the routine you and your children devise, when a child asks for help, you can revisit the routine using language like this: "Your pencil is broken? No worries. Remember how we decided to fix this problem? You [name the routine]. I trust you to do the right thing."

Gracefully
OWL

By: Violet

I watch you as you
thru the sky
gracefully
gracefully

flying into the sky
gracefully
gracefully

Sticky Notes

I asked teachers, "Would a 'need a note, get a note' policy work here, too?" They thought it would be more like a "need some, get some" policy, because kids can't use just one!

Do you sometimes read with a pencil in your hand? Maybe it's your book-club book, and you mark a passage that's confusing or one you want to share. Or maybe it's an article, and you find yourself agreeing or disagreeing, asking questions, making connections, or just wanting to remember something in particular. You write, and sometimes even draw, right there on the page. But when the book isn't yours, you just might use sticky notes instead. Students can't write in most of their books. But they can use sticky notes to make meaning, just like we do.

Acknowledge the Problem.	Ask, "What Concerns Do We Have?"	Let Go: Create an Action-Oriented, Positively Worded Question.
Routines for managing sticky notes are complicated and time-consuming.	How many do children need?	How might I show children how and why they might use sticky notes?
Teachers give out one or two at a time to individual students, usually for a specific purpose.	If I give children more, how can I make sure they will use them in appropriate ways?	How can we cocreate authentic, student-centered routines for managing sticky notes?
If children need more, they need to ask the teacher.	How can I keep from getting interrupted by children asking for more?	How can I support—and trust—children to take what they need, when they need it?

Teachers thought it was best to introduce children to sticky notes gradually because they wanted to ensure they'd use the notes in authentic, purposeful ways that would support children as readers, not as some kind of now-and-again novelty.

One of the best ways to introduce sticky notes is during one-on-one conferences. Here are a few examples:

✤ ***To the child who is having trouble remembering the same word again and again***: I say, "That word, *breathe*, is such a tricky word, isn't it? Let me write it on a sticky note so you can look at it closely. Can you read it? Now close your eyes. What letters do you see? Take a picture of it in your mind. Got it? Can you see the letters? Yes? Can you spell it? Wow. That really worked for you, didn't it? How about you keep this sticky note—you own this word, *breathe*, now, right? Do you think you might do this with other words that are tricky? I'll leave you this little stack of sticky notes just in case." And then, I encourage this child to explain what he learned about himself as a reader of tricky words during share time and ask if there is anyone else who thinks he or she might like to try his strategy tomorrow. And though I put some sticky notes at their tables the next day, the message isn't, "We're all going to do this now." It's an invitation to those who might want or need to try it and figure out whether or not this particular strategy helps them remember tricky words.

✤ ***To the child who is having trouble finding where she left off in her book***: I say, "You know how I use one of those little sticky notes to mark my place? Do you want to try it and see if it works for you? Put it on the edge of the page, like this, so a little bit sticks out. Then you just put your finger under the sticky note to find where you left off." I tell her that I don't think everyone knows about this and ask if she would be willing to show the class what she learned about herself as a reader today.

✤ ***To the child who is reading a book about the life cycle of frogs and is having trouble remembering each phase***: I say, "You know what I do to help me remember important things like this? I use a bigger sticky note with no lines on it like this one, and I draw and label what I want to remember. There's something about the drawing and the writing that helps me understand and remember it. Do you want to try it? You might want to describe each phase on one sticky note. Let's do a little bit together, and then you can figure out if this is something that works for you. I can't wait to hear what you find out."

Take a look at this email exchange between another teacher and me. Sarah had a "this is not who I am" moment. And wouldn't you know, it was doling out the sticky notes that got her thinking, too.

Hi Debbie,

I gave up my sticky note control . . . yay! My first graders did awesome! I did the same asking questions lesson that you did in KC in Grain Valley. I couldn't believe how excited they were and how the level of questioning grew throughout the week. Thank you for inspiring me to "let go" control and allow and encourage them to be independent learners. We now have a sticky note tub that is always full of sticky notes. They absolutely love showing their thinking on sticky notes without MY limits. ☺

Thank you again!

Sarah Mead (Park Hill)

- -

Hi Sarah!

I knew you'd give this a try! And don't you think so much of this is also about student engagement?

What strikes me about what you wrote is how the level of questioning grew over the course of the week, simply because students had access to as many sticky notes as they needed. So can we conclude that limiting the number of sticky notes not only diminishes student ownership and agency, but also limits student thinking? It might be fun and interesting to document this—maybe meet with a few kids (or even everyone?) and ask them to line up their questions in the order they asked them. Ask them (and yourself), "What do you notice about your questions? How did they change over time? What does this mean for us as readers and learners?"

It would be great if you'd share what you learned with teachers when we meet again in March—what do you think?

The pictures of those happy faces really say it all. Thank you so much for sharing—I can't wait to hear what you find out, and what you'll try next! See you soon!

Debbie

P.S. And can't you just envision an ongoing anchor chart that highlights all the ways/purposes children in your room use sticky notes? There could be a column for the actual sticky note and the child's name, and another column for its purpose, and how it helped this reader.

A conversation about supplies and agency

When children have learned a variety of ways readers use sticky notes, it's time to create authentic, student-centered routines for managing this classroom staple. Teachers wondered:

❖ Where will we keep our sticky notes so that everyone can get some when they need some?

❖ How will we take care of them?

❖ What if we run out?

At our next meeting, one teacher shared her class' solution:

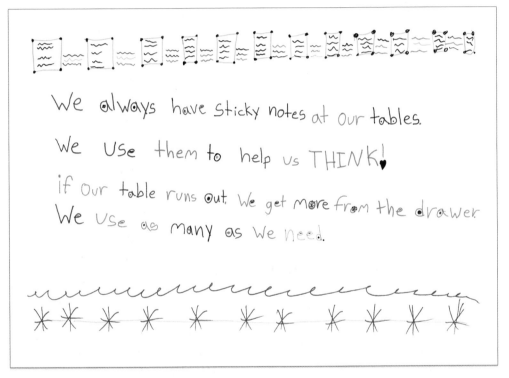

We always have sticky notes at our tables.
We use them to help us THINK!
if our table runs out, we get more from the drawer
We use as many as we need.

Eliot's synthesis of class sticky note routine serves as a belief statement and a reminder!

Teachers learned that as time went on, and the routine was firmly in place, sticky notes became a natural, everyday tool for engaging readers, making thinking visible, and showing what they knew in a range of unique and individual ways. This is all about children developing agency and figuring out what works for them. Yes, children respond in other ways, but the sticky note is always at the ready, accessible to anyone who wants one. Or two. Or six.

I see Frankie over at her desk with this long string of sticky notes. She's reading *A Kiss for Little Bear,* by Else Minarek. Curious, I head over. "Tell me about your work," I ask. She explains that she's having trouble remembering how to read some of the words that name the characters, so she's writing the word and drawing a picture until she knows the words by heart. I tell her that's such a good idea and that I do something like that, too. When I'm reading a book and I'm having difficulty keeping all the characters straight—especially in the beginning—I often write down their names in the book and a little bit about them to help me remember who is who.

Where Children Read, Write, and Talk During Work Time

Remember this research from earlier in the book?

*Providing students with choices about what to read, **where to read**, and with whom produced an impact on reading achievement more than three times as large as reported for systematic phonics instruction alone. (Guthrie and Humenick 2004; emphasis mine)*

But I don't think this means that providing students choices about where to read is about daily rotations of reading spots, drawing names out of a can, or children randomly choosing a spot.

I believe it's about children getting to know who they are as learners and readers, being aware of the task at hand, and choosing a place to read that reflects their reading and learning needs on any given day.

Just as we do.

Acknowledge the Problem.	Ask, "What Concerns Do I Have?"	Let Go: Create an Action-Oriented, Positively Worded Question.
Routines for managing where children will read and work during work time are complicated and time-consuming.	How can I make it fair?	How can I show and teach children how to choose a place to read that's based on what they need as readers on any given day?
Children have assigned spots around the room that rotate every day.	How can I stop children from racing to certain spots and pouting (and not reading) when they don't get the spot they want?	How can I trust—and support—children as they make their decisions, understanding and remembering this is a worthwhile process that will take time and patience?
The teacher draws children's names from a container, and children choose their spots one at a time.	Is my routine more about *where* children will sit than it is about reading?	
Children randomly choose a spot.	My kids aren't ready to choose where to read. How can I help them?	
Children have assigned seats. (This isn't time consuming, but children have no choice.)		

Reading spaces don't have to be fancy or themed—there's beauty in the simplicity of a small rug below a window, a little nook behind a low bookshelf, a chair that rocks or a comfy one over in the corner, a low table with pillows, a high table with stools, and even a clean and uncluttered desk. It's about children having the kinds of spaces they need to learn and grow. It's not about the spot. It's about the reader. With the right book, reading is joyful and engaging, all by itself. Let's first think about the children; next, getting great books into their hands; and finally, having a place for all children to do the work readers do in the world. Readers in the world read, write, create, and talk. We'll want space in our classrooms for children to do all those things, whether they're working independently, with a partner, or in a small group.

What if for the first three or four weeks of school, all children are sitting at their tables or desks? During this time they're learning about classroom routines and how to choose and talk about books. Children are getting to know you and each other, and you're getting to know them. You're building relationships during conferences and throughout the day, helping them understand that you trust them and hoping they trust you. And then slowly, as you confer, you can invite children to try new places to read based on what you're noticing and learning about them as learners and readers.

Here are some suggestions you might make:

❧ *To the child who is distracted by what's going on around him*: "You're working so hard learning to read this book—do you think you need a quieter spot? You do? How about moving to the little rug by the bookshelf, or over by the door? See if that helps, OK?"

❧ *To the child who is reading the same book as another child*: "Did you know Cora is reading *Each Kindness* too? There's so much to think about in that book. Maybe the two of you could find a cozy spot where you could read and talk, a place where you won't have to worry about distracting your friends. Do you want to ask her?"

❧ *To the small group of children who are all reading books by Jeanette Winter*: "It looks like you three need some room to spread out all your stuff! Do you all want to move to the meeting area to read, work, and talk quietly?"

The teachers and I talked about making sure that when we introduced where children might choose to read in these ways, we'd keep the emphasis on what children *needed* as readers on any given day and not on the spot itself. The spot should serve children. In time, we might say at the end of our lesson, "Think about what you need to do as a reader today. Where do you think you can do it best?"

▨ Designing Agentive Environments

We create agentive classroom environments to serve children and inspire the choices they make. Whether it's the books they'll read, where they'll do their best work, or what they'll make, we want to give children a range of options that invite them in and allow them to try. They'll grow into environments like these—they'll need to experiment, to learn about themselves and figure out who they are as readers and people, and what they need to be successful. Environments that are literate, organized, accessible, and authentic nurture agency, ownership, and independence.

Photos by Barb Smith

Leia during work time

Leia is also in Emily Callahan's class and she's been studying Malala Yousafzai. The goal she's set for herself today is to organize and synthesize what she's learned about Malala so far into a timeline. She has a vision of the timeline in her head and sets about getting what she needs:

- ❖ the books she's read, including *For the Right to Learn: Malala Yousafzai's Story*; *Malala, a Brave Girl from Pakistan*; *Dear Malala, We Stand with You*; *Malala Yousafzai, Warrior with Words*, and *Free as a Bird: The Story of Malala*

- ❖ reader's notebook

- ❖ three-by-three-inch sticky notes

- ❖ a few pencils

- ❖ a fine-point pen

- ❖ a few sheets of plain white paper

- ❖ a table where she can spread things out.

If you were to describe Leia, you might use the word agentive—she knows what she wants and needs to do, and she sets herself up to do it. Did the environment support her in managing her work? Yes! Agency is not only about believing you are the kind of kid who can figure things out but also about thinking it through, making a plan, getting what you need, and taking action. Agentive environments share the following characteristics:

❧ Children have access to a range of interesting books that are organized and accessible.

❧ Children have access to a range of supplies and materials that help them learn and make their thinking visible—chart paper, sticky notes in a range of sizes and colors, tape, markers, staplers, staples, paper clips, glue, and the like.

❧ Thinking is made visible through children's work, anchor charts that highlight thinking strategies and discoveries.

❧ Children have access to spaces that match their learning needs for the day— quiet places, open spaces to spread out their stuff, nooks to work together in twos and threes, and larger spaces for small groups to come together on their own or with their teacher. These spaces are clean, uncluttered, and authentic.

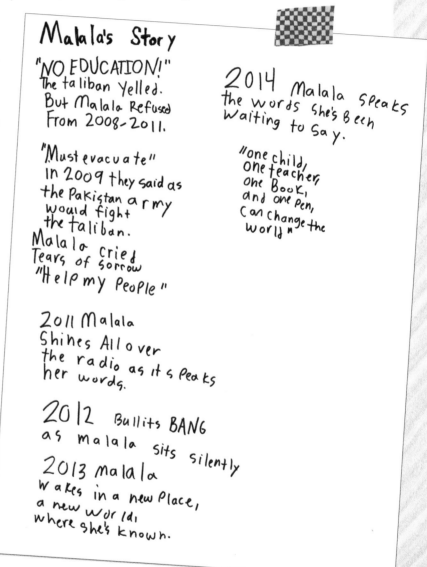

"Malala's Story," by Leia (Leia takes action!)

Agency is invitational in the beginning. "You know how you have certain spots to sit in during our minilessons? I'm thinking you're ready to start deciding for yourselves where to sit. What do you think? I'm not talking about claiming a certain spot; this is about coming to the meeting area, finding an empty spot that will work for today, and getting ready to learn with your teacher and each other, all on your own."

When we put questions like these out there, it's time to listen. Really listen. No judging allowed! Write down in your notebook or on chart paper the gist of what each child who responds has to say—recording their thinking in real time lets children know you value and respect their thinking, and it will help you remember what they said.

Take some time to think things through, then come back with a plan that incorporates their ideas and yours, and mirrors how these things work in the world. Ask the children what they think. Make adaptations as necessary, and then you might say, "Let's give this a try for a while and see how it works; we can always change our plan if we need to."

These kinds of collaborative actions promote the collective sense of agency: "We're the kind of kids—we're the kind of class—who can figure things out." Children will come up with solutions for themselves, and if those solutions don't work out, it's not the end of the world! It's simply an invitation to think about what might work better. Given that we can't predict what future world they'll have to navigate, what environments and routines they'll need to be successful, we offer them experiences with solving real problems that make a difference for their lives in the here and now and beyond. As we saw with the children in this chapter, instilling agency within children transfers to their learning.

CHAPTER 4

What If We Owned the Units We Are Asked to Teach?

Instead of thinking outside the box, innovation often involves thinking differently about the box.

—JOHN SPENCER, "THINK INSIDE THE BOX"

▨ Finding Our Way to a Beautiful Question: The Units We're Given

No one wants to be boring or bored, but sometimes the units we're given can make us feel both. My longtime friend and colleague Barb Smith, an experienced and celebrated second-grade teacher, felt that kind of dread about the upcoming Economy of Communities unit she was required to teach every year—twenty-one goals, with a new topic introduced almost daily. She found it overwhelming and underwhelming, all at the same time. Overwhelming because, like most of us, Barb isn't an economics major, plus with so many concepts to cover and a general lack of cohesion between activities, Barb wasn't sure what understandings her students would hold onto. And underwhelming

What the Research Tells Us

Research on expertise suggests that superficial coverage of many topics in the domain may be a poor way to help students develop the competencies that will prepare them for future learning and work. Curricula that emphasize breadth of knowledge may prevent effective organization of knowledge because there is not enough time to learn anything in depth. Curricula that are "a mile wide and an inch deep" run the risk of developing disconnected rather than connected knowledge. (National Research Council 2000, 42)

because the accompanying lesson plans, activities, and worksheets didn't offer the depth of understanding she knew her students were capable of.

Many units we're given have this problem. Still, we can't just dismiss them entirely. Units are created to hold us responsible to children, and provide them with a variety of rich literacy experiences, ensuring transferrable skills for their lives beyond school. They're supposed to help more teachers give all children the education they deserve. But because we're often given only one unit to envision content, we're given a limited vision of what's possible, creating the inaccurate assumption that there's only one right way to teach it.

We know that rigid systems of accountability don't help children or teachers be (or become) their best selves. But the truth is, someone else's idea of a unit doesn't have to be ours; the units we teach need to inspire us so we can inspire children—that's why we innovate and adapt. We have to trust ourselves when something feels off—we need to spend time thinking about why we feel that way. It's not that the off feeling means we should abandon the units we're given, but that we need to give ourselves some time and space to think through what is bothering us, and figure out what we'll do about it.

When we adapt the units we're given, we're being agentive; we're taking ownership of our teaching and children's learning, doing something beyond mere compliance. Maybe it would have been easier for Barb to push through and just follow the economics unit as written—I think many of us have been in this position. But Barb brought all her knowledge about teaching and learning to the unit she'd been given. She knows how to do what every good teacher needs to know—how to learn—and she knows how to teach. Take a look (right) at what Barb started to notice when she looked closely at the goals of the unit she'd been given.

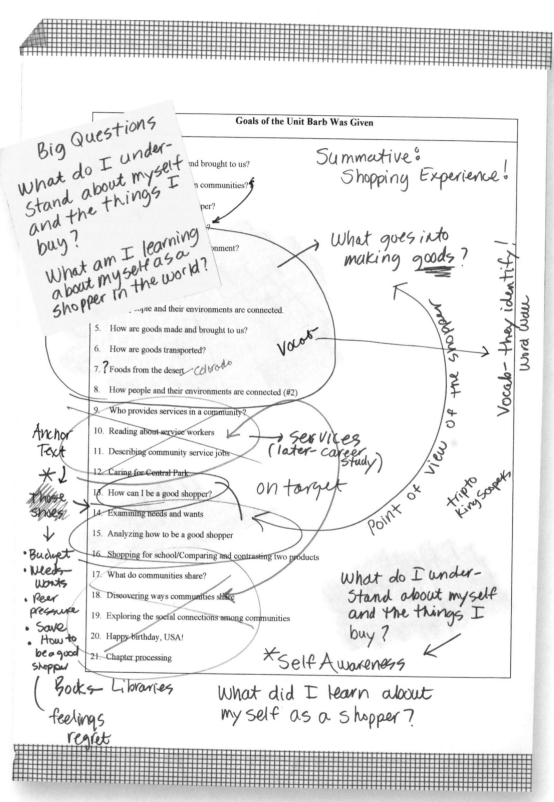

Goals of the Unit Barb Was Given

Big Questions
What do I under-stand about myself and the things I buy?

What am I learning about myself as a shopper in the world?

Summative:
Shopping Experience!

What goes into making goods?

Vocab—they identify!
Word Wall

Vocab

5. How are goods made and brought to us?
6. How are goods transported?
7. ? Foods from the desert — Colorado
8. How people and their environments are connected (#2)
9. Who provides services in a community?
10. Reading about service workers
11. Describing community service jobs
12. Caring for Central Park
13. How can I be a good shopper?
14. Examining needs and wants
15. Analyzing how to be a good shopper
16. Shopping for school/Comparing and contrasting two products
17. What do communities share?
18. Discovering ways communities share
19. Exploring the social connections among communities
20. Happy birthday, USA!
21. Chapter processing

Services
(later-career study)

on target

Point of view of the shopper

Trip to King Soopers

Anchor Text
* ↓
Those Shoes
↓
• Budget
• Needs-Wants
• Peer pressure
• Save
• How to be a good shopper

Books Libraries

feelings regret

What do I under-stand about myself and the things I buy?

* Self Awareness

What did I learn about my self as a shopper?

Barb's marked-up unit. When you look closely at this page, what do you notice about Barb's thinking?

Like Barb, Karen Cangelese is also an experienced and masterful teacher, the kind of teacher who is up for almost anything as long as it is purposeful work that engages kids, gets them thinking, and makes them smarter about content and themselves as learners. Not long ago we were in her kindergarten classroom, thinking about an upcoming unit on characters in literature. Like many of us, her work is driven by her state's standards, and she works hard to place required units into meaningful contexts for children as well as remain true to her beliefs about children, teaching, and learning.

Just as Barb did, Karen looked closely at the unit to think it through and consider how she might go about teaching it. She focused on the goals of the unit first.

It didn't take Karen long to realize that her kindergartners were already able to do what was outlined in this unit—they'd had experience and practice with these concepts throughout the year, mostly through interactive read-alouds, independent work with wordless books and early readers, and conferences. She wondered, "How can I think beyond what's written here? How can I help children work with more independence than they do now? How might I create learning situations where children can grapple with *why* authors create the characters they do and *how* they get us to care about them?"

Barb and Karen helped me understand the specifics of why adaptation is a necessary response to any unit we've been given. While the degree of adaptation varies depending on the needs of our children, the expectation that we reframe the units we're given is always there. And this is what great teaching is, right? We work from what we know to be true about teaching, about reading, and about children and go from there—we're always charged with adapting what we've been given so that we can best meet the needs of the children in front of us. There's no one magic unit that we can, or even should, repeat in the exact same way every year. (Even that favorite koala, penguin, or rain forest unit!)

With prompting and support, identify characters, settings, and major events in a story.

- Develop and apply skills to the reading process.

- Comprehend

- With assistance, develop and demonstrate reading skills in response to read-alouds by:
  - *recognizing beginning, middle, and end.*

With prompting and support, describe the connection between two individuals, events, ideas, or pieces of information in a text.

- Develop and apply skills to the reading process.

- Make connections

- With assistance, determine the connection between:
  - *text-to-text (text ideas, including similarities and differences in fiction and nonfiction).*

With prompting and support, compare and contrast the adventures and experiences of characters in familiar stories.

- Develop and apply skills and strategies to comprehend, analyze and evaluate fiction, poetry, and drama from a variety of cultures and times.

- With assistance, read, infer, and draw conclusions to:
  - *Identify elements of a story, including setting, character, and key events.*
  - *Compare and contrast adventures of characters in familiar stories.*

How does understanding the characters, setting, and key events help us to clarify what we just read?

How does understanding the adventures and experiences of characters help to clarify what we just read?

I can describe the adventures and experiences of characters in a story.

I can explain how the adventures and experiences of characters are alike and different.

character	experience
setting	compare
key event	contrast
adventure	

Goals of unit Karen was given

Barb and Karen were provoked by challenging units they'd been given and realized that the units couldn't be taught as they were. Here are some of the common problems we identified:

Common Problems with the Units We're Given

❖ The unit covers more content than children can learn in a deep and abiding way. The unit gives only superficial exposure to the skills. The unit asks children to learn the skills but doesn't show why the skills matter to them.

❖ The unit repeats content children already know.

❖ The unit has a topic and a collection of questions, but the questions aren't open-ended or connected strongly enough. Learning doesn't transfer often enough from one activity to the next, and so the unit is more a collection of ideas, rather than a coherent conceptual framework.

❖ The unit doesn't give children an authentic, relevant experience for synthesizing and transferring their final understanding of the skills. There's no summative assessment, so teachers and children aren't sure where they are headed or what they're working toward. It's hard to plan a series of connected lessons when we don't know where we're going.

❖ The unit doesn't include the reading, writing, and talking opportunities necessary to develop the background knowledge, content, and reading skills of the specific children we have in our class.

❖ The unit doesn't describe how to use time in a way that allows for the in-class independent work time and conferring that we know make learning effective.

Barb and Karen named the problems, faced their discomfort, rolled up their sleeves, and decided to ask this beautiful question: "What if we owned the units we're asked to teach?" Let's learn from Barb and Karen and hold onto some of the big thinking they did to take ownership of their given units for their students and for themselves. Over the next few pages, you'll see how Barb and Karen became more agentive teachers who trusted themselves enough not to just go along, but to try to figure out how to make things better. Not perfect. Better.

Barb and Karen know that the act and the art of teaching is itself a constant state of learning: we assess what children need and we adapt to meet those needs. When we're in full adaptation mode, that "this doesn't feel right" feeling fades away—we're taking action to make it better; we're doing all we can. The power is ours to take. We know that throwing units out can be risky, but let's see how adapting them can be genius.

How to Take Ownership of a Unit (Lessons from Barb and Karen)

Ask, "**Are these the right goals for my students?** Can I cluster some of them? What's the most interesting and important idea or learning in this unit? How can I adapt it (deepen it or scaffold it) to better meet my children where they are and help them grow?" We decide what children need most and go with it. Can these goals be gathered under one or just a few big ideas or questions that are worth holding onto? Can we invite children to think and learn about this topic in ways that will endure beyond this unit so that they see today's work matters not just now but for their whole lives?

Ask, "**Which texts work best?** How can I assemble a diverse collection of texts so that children have multiple accessible examples of the big ideas in this unit? Can literature and nonfiction work together to help illustrate big ideas about the content areas? What knowledge is new for my students and how do I help them hold onto that?"

Ask, "**How can this fit within the daily workshop structure?** Given that we know the structure of workshop maximizes children's learning by providing brief targeted instruction, plenty of independent work time, and individualized conferring, how can I adjust the rhythm of the unit so that it flows within readers' workshop?"

Ask, "**How will we know when we're done?** What do I want my students to be able to do [real-world product, performance, or application] at the end of the unit? And why does doing this matter?" It needs to exist in the real world and have a real-world audience. We want content knowledge and skill development to come together in one or more authentic experiences that will stick with children not just for this year, but for years to come.

Note: If you are familiar with the work of Grant Wiggins and Jay McTighe (*Understanding by Design,* 2005), you'll notice some overlap, but here I focused on what's really necessary for improving an existing unit. For more on Wiggins and McTighe and their work, consider reading their book *The Understanding by Design Guide to Creating High-Quality Units* (2011). Also, Sam Bennett's *That Workshop Book: New Systems and Structures for Classrooms That Read, Write, and Think* (2007) will give you additional insights into planning units and embedding them within a readers' workshop.

Dear Reader, If you're given a unit to teach, and it doesn't feel quite right, know that you're not alone. You can make some changes, just like Barb and Karen did, as you'll see in the pages that follow. You don't have to change everything; ask yourself, "What feels doable right now?" Maybe it's going to the library and bringing in more books for children to read, write, and talk about. Maybe it's asking a big, beautiful question to guide you and your children in their work. Maybe it's placing a social studies unit in your readers' workshop. Or maybe, if the unit doesn't have a summative experience to work toward, you can decide on one. (It could be as simple as inviting the children across the hall to come in for twenty minutes to learn from your kids.) Any one of these is a step toward teacher ownership and agency. Any step you take to own a unit and make it better is a powerful one. You owe it to kids, and you owe it to yourself too. You'll see some space in the pages that follow for you to try some changes for a unit you've been given. Let yourself have fun considering what's possible!

–Debbie

▨ Are These the Right Goals?

When Barb clustered the goals of the unit she'd been given, she asked, "What's an interesting, big idea here? Is there a bigger, simpler understanding embedded within all these goals?" Barb realized that many of the goals were from the perspective of the consumer or shopper and thought this might be the big idea she was looking for. She could have gone in several directions, such as community

services or service workers, but Barb felt that focusing on consumers—how and why they make the decisions they do—would be most interesting, relevant, and engaging for her children this year.

Barb's Goals for Children

❖ Learn how to become a thoughtful shopper and consumer.

❖ Understand how to make smart decisions and develop personal considerations.

❖ Use thinking strategies to make meaning.

❖ Understand how study groups help us grow.

Karen decided to invite children to consider the larger purposes of reading and what purpose characters serve, because she knew this would lead them not only to identify characters, describe their feelings, compare and contrast adventures, and think about what the author wanted them to remember, but also to become friends with them, learn from and with them, and even advise them.

So Karen asked herself: "How might children and I take this unit deeper? How can I help them work with more independence than they do now? How might I create learning situations where children will grapple with *why* authors create the characters they do and *how* they get us to care about them?" She followed that wondering and asked, "Maybe instead of learning about characters from many books by different authors, kids could dig deep into an author study where children would develop a lasting relationship with one author and the characters he or she writes about?" Could she honor the thinking that had gone into the creation of the unit she'd been given and take it in a direction that better suited the children in her classroom? Of course she could.

Karen's children loved Mo Willems; they would be coming to their character unit with genuine passion and would wonder, "How does Mo Willems *do* it? How does he make us love his characters so much?" By focusing on just one author, Karen thought it might be easier to understand how and why authors create the characters they do—what do they want their characters to teach readers? This might seem heady for kindergartners, but Karen knew they'd be up for it; this was going to be an immersive, authentic experience that would allow children to dig into books they could read and think, write, and draw about on their own and with friends and share about with everyone during reflection time.

Karen's Goals for Children

❖ Develop a relationship with Mo Willems, the characters he creates, and the books he writes.

❖ Use thinking strategies independently to make meaning.

❖ Use what they know about letters, sounds, and words to read Mo Willems' books independently.

Barb and Karen decided to collect their goals into questions that children could hold onto as they learned throughout the unit. (This idea of an overarching question comes from the *Understanding by Design* model [Wiggins and McTighe 2005].) Without questions that engage children, the kinds of questions that invite them to consider more than even we can imagine, we get conformity and compliance. But when we put forward big, beautiful questions, we're asking children to be creative and make meaning.

Children don't develop agency by being told what to do and how to do it, step by step by step. They develop agency by working hard to discover and figure things out in a variety of ways.

These were Barb's beautiful questions for her children:

❖ What do I understand about myself and the things I buy?

❖ What am I learning about myself as a shopper in the world?

❖ Do study groups really make me smarter, more interesting, and more interested in the world and other people? What can I give? What can I get?

These questions seem very different from those in the unit Barb was given! They're interesting questions that were actionable, were specific to her children, and would give them something to think and talk about. And through what children would read, write, and talk about and Barb's minilessons, they'd be able to answer them in a variety of ways. And here's how Karen transformed her

Guiding Question in the Original Unit	Guiding Questions in Karen's Revision
How does understanding the adventures and experiences of characters help us clarify what we just read?	**What is in the author's heart? How does she or he show us?** **How does what I'm reading influence how I read it?** **How do characters in stories help us become better human beings?**

Guiding questions

Reimagine a Unit

The Right Goals for Your Students Right Now

Question(s) That Puts the Goals in Authentic Context

----

given unit to make it relevant for this year's children.

Take a look back to see how Barb's and Karen's questions collected their goals and offered children something to hold onto. The goals stated what we thought was important for the children in their classrooms; the questions gave children a reason to pursue those goals each day. Want to try it? Consider a unit that makes you feel blah or anxious. Take ownership! Use Barb's and Karen's guidelines for reimagining a unit as a better teaching and learning experience for you and your students.

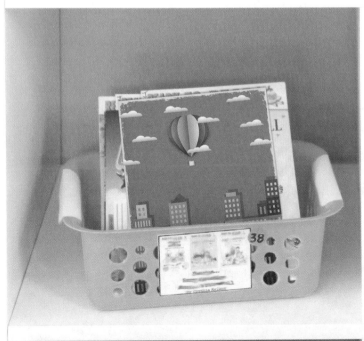

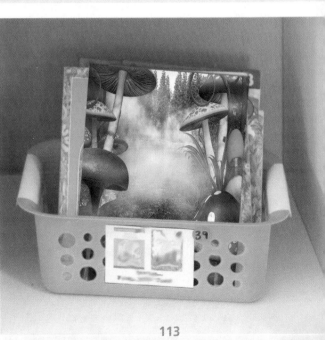

▓▓ Which Texts Work Best?

Other than a set of social studies textbooks, Barb's classroom library didn't have many books about economics, and neither did her school library. Barb knows that kids need to choose from a wide range of texts, so she went to two public libraries, searching for books that children could read that would be interesting, give them something to think and talk about, and of course build their background knowledge about economics. While she managed to find sixty or so books, many of them weren't as engaging as the reading children normally did. But they *were* full of useful information, and because the children's reading was framed by an authentic reason to read, and lots of partner reading and thinking, children became engaged.

You might think Barb would be done gathering books for this unit, but not quite. Because this unit was primarily about self-awareness, reflection, and learning about themselves as consumers and shoppers in the world, she wanted an anchoring text—a great story with believable characters that kids could connect to, engage with, learn from, and talk about. This is an example of the genius thinking Barb brought to reimaging this unit. Yes, it was a content area study—economics—but literature could also be relevant. We don't need to rely solely on nonfiction to teach the content areas! The book *Those Shoes*, by Maribeth Boelts (2007), came to mind, and Barb found it was the perfect choice! Stories like this one bring content to life, giving children rich contexts for discussion and learning.

As Barb read the book to herself, she jotted some of the big ideas and questions in her notebook, specifically those that connected to children's goals and big questions. This helped her plan lessons and study-group discussions, and though she would also encourage children to ask their own questions, she knew she needed to know the book well to maximize its impact. Books like *Those Shoes* allow children and teachers to dig deeper into a topic, connect with the characters, and think about big ideas and concepts that informational texts (at least those she found on this topic) don't typically offer. When we're teaching children content, we can have opportunities and responsibilities to teach and show them what it means to be human and citizens of the world.

Here are some of the big ideas she found in this short and beautiful picture book:

❖ We all have dreams of things we want. (Even if we have the money, should we have everything we want? Are there enough resources in the world for that to happen?)

❖ There is a difference between needs and wants. (From the picture, what do you know about what Jeremy's Grandma needs? What does this tell us about what's important to her? Are people's needs and wants different? Could one person's needs be another person's wants? What about the other way around?)

❖ "Everybody has them." (Is that a good reason to buy something?)

❖ What is peer pressure?

❖ Does wanting something so badly make it more important than it really is? Is it more about having to have it than really needing it? Or even wanting it? What questions might we ask ourselves to help us decide?

❖ Is it smart to buy something similar that costs less money? Should you buy something that doesn't fit or work just right because you want it so much?

❖ How are you like Jeremy? How are the two of you different?

❖ Have you ever regretted buying something you thought you really wanted? Tell the story to your group. What did you learn?

❖ Have you ever given away something you loved to someone who needed it more? How did that feel? Would you do it again?

❖ Are the things we already have worth more than the things we want?

What do I want kids to be able to do at the end of the unit? Why does this matter?

How will I ground content knowledge and skill development so that it will stick?

Sat.
¶ Get Books
Denver Public Library
Ross Library - UHills
720-865-1111
720 865-0955

Books on economics
5 copies - Those Shoes

Gather -
...ils, markers
...l toys, jacks,
...l glue sticks
...rck, etc
...pping el-
...ue - ask
..., ...ory, Theo...

* Form study groups Friday - before unit

* Chant for Those Shoes - Big Ideas from kids...

* Vocab wall - where? ongoing...

What do I understand about myself and the things I buy?

What am I learning about myself as a shopper in the world?

M	T	W	Th	F
Week 1 Intro Those Shoes - Study groups - discussion of needs/wants - why this study matters. Ind. reading - read, write, talk w/a partner - what strategies do we know to use? Lessons on asking ?s and det. importance. Vocab - ongoing wall - Friday				
Week 2 Balance study groups - independent content reading. Focus on goods - how made & brought to us - why does this matter? How does this affect my shopping decisions - or does it? Should it? Comprehension - inferring - synthesis				
Week 3 Study group - What is a shopping mindset? List 9 what to think about... Walking trip to King Soopers - how do merchants lure shoppers? Will you/ would you "fall for it."				Friday - Let's go shopping! Capplication of learning

Barb's thinking about her reimagined unit

Once Karen had committed to an author study, she asked herself, "Out of all of the books children are reading and listening to, which ones contain memorable and interesting characters that they love, delight in, and connect with most?" She knew the answer right away—the characters her children loved and talked about most had names like Pigeon, Gerald, Piggie, Duckling, Trixie, City Dog, and Country Frog, all from books written by one author, Mo Willems.

It was the final quarter of the year, and children were able to read many of these books independently or with the support of a partner. She decided to build on children's interests and create an author study of Mo Willems, embedding a character study within it, giving Pigeon, Gerald, Piggie, Trixie, and all their friends a place to come alive and live, love, and grow in children's hearts and minds.

Karen gathered as many of Mo Willems' books as she could, including persuading children to relinquish (just for now!) any squirreled-away copies at school and at home, raiding several nearby libraries, asking other teachers to share their collections with her, and making an after-school run to the used bookstore down the street. In a week's time, Karen and her children had access to over two hundred books by Mo Willems! (They could have done with fewer books, but this way they could access almost any book they wanted, and there were multiple copies for children to read with a partner, in small groups, or in whatever ways they believed would suit them best.)

Karen and a friend read and talked their way through as many as they could one afternoon after school, and they found themselves doing the following:

- ❖ noticing how important the illustrations were to the stories—they were instrumental in helping readers infer what the characters were thinking and feeling;

- ❖ identifying with characters;

- ❖ learning about themselves and each other through character interactions;

- ❖ connecting themes and big ideas across texts;

- ❖ inferring what Mo Willems wanted readers to think about and remember;

- ❖ empathizing with characters, identifying patterns, and stepping into the stories;

- ❖ predicting as they read, as well as making predictions about what a Mo Willems book was going to be about based on its title and their knowledge of the characters featured; and

- ❖ wanting to work together rather than independently.

Your text choice and thinking around the texts can make a big difference to a unit. Which texts do you think will serve children best?

Reimagine a Unit

Your Choice of Texts

- -

- -

- -

Your Noticing of the Big Ideas in These Texts

- -

- -

- -

▨ How Will We Know When We're Done?

Many of the units we're given lack a summative experience, performance, or celebration of all that children have accomplished, and teachers and children aren't quite sure where they're headed; sometimes the only way we know we're done is when we run out of lessons. It's like one unit isn't even in the books before we are asked to begin the next one, often the very next day. Wait a minute! We've been working two, three, four weeks or more on a single topic, and then one day we're just *done*? How will we show what we know? Whom do we get to share with? How do we celebrate our hard work and learning?

Barb had goals for her students, regular authentic experiences, and a meaningful question, but what authentic experience could bring all that learning over time together? What did Barb want her children to know and be able to do at the end of the unit? Because her reimagined unit was all about students becoming

aware of themselves as shoppers and consumers, she envisioned a real shopping experience (or as real as you can get with ten dollars' worth of play money!) where children would have opportunities to transfer what they'd learned about what they, and shoppers in the world, think about and do. She envisioned tables set up throughout the classroom, filled with small toys and games, notebooks, pencils, candy, books, stuffed animals, markers, paper clips, folders, little bouncy balls, and more. She wanted children to have opportunities to buy from tables with items labeled $1, $2, $5, and $10, applying what they'd learned about how shoppers make smart decisions that are just right for them. (Parents donated some of the items, and Barb and fellow teachers scoured around for the rest.)

Barb was intentional with the items children could buy as well as the amount of money she planned to give them—she hoped they would consider their newfound knowledge about needs and wants, peer pressure, and where and how things were made, and shop with an awareness of how and why they made their decisions. Afterward she envisioned them reflecting and sharing with their study groups and the whole class about what they'd learned: What did they notice or learn about themselves as shoppers? Did their shopping experience go the way they thought it would? Did any of their actions or purchases surprise them? Did they feel pressure to buy something because someone else did? What were they proud of?

Barb's shopping experience

Photos by Barb Smith

Why did this study matter? Barb's kids were only seven and eight. But we hear again and again that economics is an integral part of our lives, and an understanding of it is critical in helping people comprehend the modern world and make decisions that shape the future. So why not create a shopping experience where children could apply what they had learned and reflect on themselves as consumers in the world and how they were forming their shopping decisions? It was a start. And I can't wait to see what Barb does with the unit next year and the year after that!

Kids reflect on their shopping experience.

Photos by Barb Smith

When Karen thought about how students could celebrate all their learning, she envisioned the author study of Mo Willems becoming a child-created "MOseum" in their classroom—children's work, photos, and learning would be featured on foldable screens; tables would be filled with Mo's books; walls would be covered with charts that documented children's thinking. She pictured an evening affair, with children guiding their families through their MOseum, explaining what was in Mo's heart, sharing their learning about the characters he wrote about, and explaining what they had learned about themselves as readers, writers, thinkers, and people in the world. And, oh yes—she envisioned Pigeon cookies with icing!

Mo Willems INSPIRES us to be authors!

The Pigeon's Emotions
Frustrated Happy Sad Bad Attitude

While the Pigeon has many emotions, he is always HAPPY at the end!

Photos by Karen Cangelose

Welcome to our MOseum!

How might you help students recognize all that they've learned in a unit you've been given? Making it fun, joyful, and real? Sometimes a teacher might just take ownership of a unit by starting here. That's extremely worthwhile in and of itself. Children are often unaware of what they've learned, unfortunately, let alone given the opportunity to celebrate, so let them take joyful ownership of all that learning by offering them an experience that lets them showcase what they know!

Reimagine a Unit

Your Summative, Celebratory Experience

- -

- -

- -

- -

- -

- -

 ## How Can This Happen Within Daily Workshop?

Many units we're given are a collection of lessons. When it comes to teaching content studies, many teachers have a thirty-or-so-minute period two or three days a week allocated for social studies and science. When this is the case, we often resort to telling children about a topic, or reading aloud to them, thinking that somehow that is enough. I know all about this, because I used to do that too. But I know more now than I did then. While the lessons can be helpful in providing examples of the specific language we can use to talk about the content, telling isn't teaching. Children also need lots of books about the topic, and time to read, write, and talk—all to make meaning for themselves and each other. Teachers need time for conferring with individual children, partnerships, and small groups, as well as time for explicit teaching through minilessons.

The workshop is the perfect format for all of these things! And children will get smarter not only about content but also about text structures, comprehension, and how to effectively participate in a study group. Barb plans for content studies the same way she plans for all workshops: identify the focus of the lesson—the learning target; plan the work time; plan the minilesson; plan the share.

A list of some of Barb's learning targets are on the following page. Once Barb got into the unit and learned more about students and their needs, she'd refine, add, or delete some of them, but this gave her a place to begin. You'll notice that the targets aren't only topic-specific; children would also be building on what they already knew about how to use comprehension strategies to access the content in their books and how to be interesting and interested participants in an economics study group. The targets are a balance between the what (economics content), the how (strategies for making meaning), and the significance of the study, or why it mattered (study group).

What the Research Tells Us

A review of the research on learning by the Committees on Developments in the Science of Learning and Learning Research and Educational Practice (Bransford 2000, 18–21) found that the most effective learning opportunities ensure that

1. The learner's preexisting understandings are identified and refined through feedback;

2. The learner explores concepts in depth and through different examples of the same concept (depth is prioritized over superficial coverage); and

3. The learner practices not only subject area skills, but metacognition, setting his or her own learning goals and self-monitoring progress.

Next up for Barb was thinking through formative assessments—she already knew she'd learn the most by conferring with and listening in to children's study groups, and that sticky notes and written reflections would also be important; she just needed to figure out what that would look like on a daily basis.

Following is one of Barb's lessons. Thinking about vocabulary this way was something new for Barb—she wondered, "Instead of me identifying the words, what if I asked children to write down the kinds of words economists use to think and talk about economies?" She knew she could add words to the list, but she thought, "Wouldn't it be interesting to find out what kids would find?"

What do you notice? What does Barb's lesson make you think about? Do you see any implications for you and your students?

Possibilities for Children's Learning Targets

I can use reading strategies to help me make meaning.

❖ I can build my background knowledge about economics to help me grow what I know.

❖ I can ask questions when I read to help me monitor my comprehension.

❖ I can determine what's important in my reading to help me make meaning.

❖ I can synthesize my learning to share with others. (I can teach someone else what I learned in my own words, in a way that makes sense, without telling too much.)

❖ I can explain how I read and learn from the texts in my stack.

I can describe ways to prepare to make my study group interesting.

❖ I can hold my thinking in a variety of ways to share with my study group.

❖ I can share my thinking and learning in my own words.

❖ I can find evidence in the text to support my thinking.

❖ I can get smarter with my friends. (What can I give? What can I get?)

I can build my background knowledge about economics and myself as a shopper.

❖ I can identify vocabulary specific to economics.

❖ I can explain the difference between needs and wants.

❖ I can explain how goods are made and brought to us. I can explain why this matters.

❖ I can identify where different things in my home are made. (Homework/ share in workshop opening/What did we notice? What surprised us?)

❖ I can explain how to compare similar products and why it matters.

❖ I can observe how, where, and why goods are displayed. What will I watch out for? (Walking field trip to King Soopers, a local grocery store)

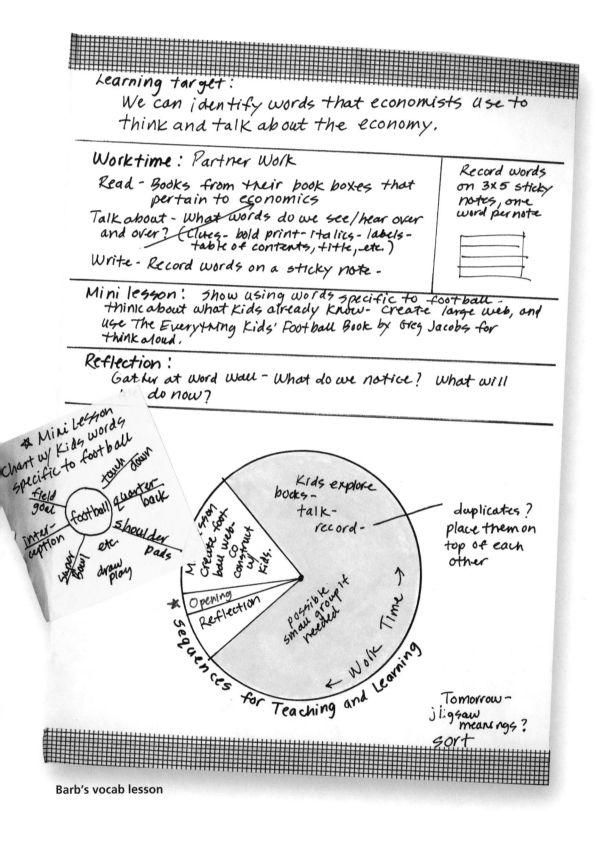

Learning target:
We can identify words that economists use to think and talk about the economy.

Worktime: Partner Work

Read - Books from their book boxes that pertain to economics

Talk about - What words do we see/hear over and over? (Clues- bold print- italics- labels- table of contents, title, etc.)

Write - Record words on a sticky note -

Record words on 3x5 sticky notes, one word per note

Mini lesson: Show using words specific to football - think about what kids already know - create large web, and use The Everything Kids' Football Book by Greg Jacobs for think aloud.

Reflection:
Gather at word wall - What do we notice? What will [we] do now?

★ Mini Lesson
Chart w/ kids words specific to football
field goal — football — touch down — quarter back — interception — super bowl — draw play — etc. — shoulder pads

Opening
Reflection
Create football web- co-construct w/ kids.
Kids explore books- talk- record-
possible small group if needed
← Work Time →
sequences for Teaching and Learning

duplicates? place them on top of each other

Tomorrow- jigsaw meanings? sort

Barb's vocab lesson

Karen's given unit also didn't include guidelines for workshop, so she created a list of possible learning targets and formative assessments for this four-week author study. Placed within readers' workshop, each of these targets would move children closer to where they were headed—the MOseum, their final demonstration of understanding. Just like Barb's learning targets, Karen's were fluid.

Possible Learning Targets	Possible Formative Assessments
I can use thinking strategies to help me make meaning.	• Conferring
I can build my background knowledge about Mo Willems and the stories he writes.	• Anchor charts (ongoing)
I can make connections from a character(s) in one book to a character(s) in another book.	• Listening in to student conversations
I can make personal connections to some of the characters in the books I'm reading.	• Whole-group and small-group discussions
I can infer big ideas and themes in stories I read.	• Share and reflection time
I can retell the stories I read.	• Thinking sheets
	• Teacher observations
I can explain what I learned about Mo Willems and the characters in his books.	• Conferring
I can identify characters, settings, and big events in a story.	• Anchor charts
I can describe the characters in Mo Willems' books.	• Listening in to student conversations
I can predict what certain characters will think, say, do, and feel.	• Whole-group and small-group discussions
I can identify which character is most like me and explain why.	• Share and reflection time
I can explain what I know in a voice that others can hear and understand.	• Thinking sheets
I can explain what's in Mo Willems' heart.	• Teacher observations
	• MOseum participation

To get a glimpse of what some of Karen's lessons looked like, I documented some of them for her—things happen so fast in the classroom that we can lose sight of all the work we do and all that children can do. Documenting a lesson gives us great opportunities to pause a moment and reflect on what we do and why we do it. I used to do this in my own classroom, particularly during work

Possible Learning Targets (cont.)	Possible Formative Assessments (cont.)
I can use what I know about letters, sounds, and words to read books.	• Conferring
I can use a variety of strategies to help me figure out unknown words.	• Listening in to students' conversations
I can reread books to help me remember new words, understand stories, and read fluently.	• Teacher observations
I can read a story aloud fluently and with expression.	• MOseum read-aloud
I can explain how I'm smarter now than I was before.	• Conferring
I can explain what I learned about myself as a reader.	• Reflection and share time
I can explain what I learned about myself as a person.	• MOseum participation
I can explain what I learned about Mo Willems and the books he writes.	• Looking across children's thinking sheets, conferring notes, and teacher observation
I can explain how I know.	

Learning targets and assessments

time—I'd put myself in documentary mode, make sure my phone was charged, and snap away, photographing and capturing kids at work. The trick was getting the photos off my phone and into my notebook, but when I did, I loved (and love) looking back, reflecting, and remembering a day in the life. . . .

So, Karen, here's to you! Thank you for all you do for kids and teachers in North Kansas City.

And you, teacher reader, here's to you! Try some of these ideas out and see if they work for you.

M   T   W   Th   F

Big Picture Week- Building schema for Mo and what he writes, how he writes, and why he writes. Lots of read alouds, think alouds, and even more time for kids to read, talk, explore and discover.

Looking closely at characters - what do they say, do, think and feel? What have we come to expect from certain characters? What patterns do we notice? (which character is most like me?)

Reflection Week- What did Mo's characters teach us? What does he want us to remember ten years from now? What's in Mo's heart? (theme/patterns)

MOseum on Wednesday! (open house) of course!
(grade 1 am/ parents 5:30-6:30)
Displays up/ signs by kids/ table art / pigeon cookies?

Karen's workshop plans

How will kids get smarter about today's target and themselves as readers? What will they:
*Read?
   Mo Books up until the share.
   Free choice from book boxes after.

*Talk about?
   What's in Mo's ♥? What does he want us to remember 10 years from now?

*Write? Respond to question(s) above

*Why does this matter?
   This is all about what readers do in the world. We want to take all kids - even ink- beyond the surface level - reading is more than simply reading words. This shows kids how to slow down and take time- on their own or with a friend, and figure out what the author cares about and wants us to remember. This is comprehension!

*What do children need from me?
   Refer to previous lessons and "what patterns do we see?" (This gets at "How do we know?") Model only if kids need it. -Get kids talking w/a partner - listen in - who needs more support? Small group? Conference?

Reimagine a Unit

Learning Targets for Your Students

- -

- -

- -

Work Time and Formative Assessments
(Write or Draw, Talk, Read)

- -

- -

- -

What's the Best That Could Happen? Perfection in Imperfection

One tricky thing about teaching units and lessons that someone else has written is that it can put your mind, and sometimes your heart, on hold. And so of course it puts children on hold, too. We don't necessarily ask ourselves, "What's the best that can happen?" because we don't really think about the units we're given in that way. We already know—we have a fixed idea of what will happen because it's written right there on the page. It can feel like the teaching we're doing isn't really ours; it's as if we're just filling in for someone else, going down a list of lessons and doing our best. When we feel this way, we don't own the units we've been given; the units we've been given own us.

When we decide to own a unit, we take time to consider what we need to change in order to make it better. We think about what we know about children so far, and do our best to adapt the unit to best meet their needs. But adaptation is never perfect. Through each unit we teach, we learn more about our students and more about our teaching. And though it's easy to feel

defeated when things don't go according to plan, there's no need to be upset. The reality is that it will never go according to plan, because a rigid plan isn't teaching. A thoughtful plan that invites expansive possibilities is.

So the fact that our plans will change is a given! That's because we can't know exactly where kids are and the ways they will respond until we're in the middle of things. We listen, we learn, we revise. Yes, we stay true to where we're headed, to what children need to know by the end of the unit. But *how* we get there? That's another story. We're open to new possibilities that go beyond our initial thinking; we trust that children will inform and guide us along the way. And we trust ourselves and the decisions we make.

Let Barb's and Karen's examples help you consider what's possible when we take ownership of the units we're given, adapting them to offer children expansive visions of themselves. Were either of these units perfect? Barb and Karen would both say they weren't, but what unit is? And really, should perfection be our goal? If it is, we risk overscaffolding children and becoming scripty in our delivery. Maybe we need a new definition of perfection: We do the best we can. We understand that we'll need to refine and adjust our plan along the way, depending on what we're learning from the children in our care. We trust the process, and we trust kids and ourselves. And we know that every day we have the opportunity and the responsibility to be smarter about children and ourselves as teachers at the end of the day than we were at the beginning. This, my friend, is perfection.

The fire of literacy is created by the emotional sparks between a child, a book, and the person reading. It isn't achieved by the book alone, nor by the child alone, nor by the adult who's reading aloud—it's the relationship winding between all three, bringing them together in easy harmony.

—MEM FOX

READING MAGIC: WHY READING ALOUD TO OUR CHILDREN WILL CHANGE THEIR LIVES FOREVER (2001)

CHAPTER 5

What If Read-Aloud Sustained Children's Independent Thinking?

▓ Finding Our Way to a Beautiful Question: The Wisdom in Children's Thinking

It was early April when I visited Val's first-grade classroom with a group of teachers to do some demonstration teaching. Val's students were near the end of a unit that focused on asking questions in order to make meaning in literary text, and we'd decided to go beyond the basic *who, what, where,* and *when* questions and focus on deeper, more complex ones like these:

❖ Why do writers write books for us?

❖ What do they want us to think about and remember forever? (What's the author's message?)

❖ How do authors inspire us?

❖ How do books change the way(s) we see the world?

Val and I had invited children to choose a partner, find a book from those she'd read aloud throughout the year and work to figure out these questions, particularly the one about figuring out what the author wants us to think about and remember. After about thirty minutes of reading and rereading, looking closely at the pictures, and talking, children came together to share their thinking. Here's what they had to say:

"Our book is about loving, and caring, and sharing with everyone. Even a homeless man or a bird or a boy." (*A Circle of Friends*)

"We think that just because you wear fancy clothes doesn't mean you're nice. And if you wear dirty clothes it doesn't mean you're mean. It's like clothes don't really matter. It's about your heart." (*The Paper Bag Princess*)

"Solomon Singer lived in New York City, but he kept dreaming of going back home to Indiana. He wanted stuff like a cat and a balcony and purple walls. But he met a waiter named Angel at a café and Angel smiled at him every time he came back and then Solomon Singer knew he didn't really need to go to Indiana or have a balcony. He just needed a friend." (*An Angel for Solomon Singer*)

"We know if your mom has a baby, she still loves you. But babies are a lot of work and she's really busy and so she might forget a little bit about you. But you don't have to worry because it will be better in a little bit of time and we know that because that's what happened to us and Lou." (*Koala Lou*)

During the share, one after another, each first-grade pair shared heartfelt thinking about their books. They'd been able to understand the author's message and consider how that message was relevant to them. I could only respond with a question: "What are we going to do with all the important messages you've discovered?"

One child's voice made itself heard above the rest: "We should let them go," she responded. "Let them go out into the world!"

This idea was greeted with exuberant clapping and throwing of hands in the air—the rest of the children thought letting their important messages go out into the world was a good idea, too.

Teachers loved what they saw and heard, but they weren't yet clear about how all this great thinking came to be. An observer from another district wondered if this was a "gifted class or something" because how else could that many first graders articulate their thinking in such sophisticated ways?

"Yes, they're gifted," I said, "just like the children in your district are, and everyone else's in this room today." And then I explained.

1. Val had been doing daily read-alouds with interesting picture books all year long. These children saw reading as joyful and sharing their thinking about what they read as a natural community experience.

2. The books in their hands that day were picture books their teacher had read aloud (and they had discussed) multiple times throughout the year.

3. These stories generally contained clear, identifiable messages.

4. Children worked and talked with a book and a partner they'd chosen.

5. They had time—no one felt rushed.

6. Because they'd heard the books before, they were able to focus on the thinking, not the reading.

7. Val and I celebrated their thinking and invited them to do more with it.

But before we think about the *how* in more detail, let's think more about what happens when we limit what's possible for ourselves and for our students. I get why people respond to something impressive in someone else's teaching with a fearful "I can't do that because. . . ." I've had moments like that: the opening of Chapter 2 describes me pushing through one of them. I know that for me, those moments usually happen when I don't feel that confident or competent—I can't envision myself being successful.

There's also another version of I can't: "I can't do that because. . . . " We say it because we think children are too young, or too inexperienced, or somehow not ready. But each of the things that we believe children can't do risks becoming something they'll never get to do in their time with us. We can't postpone what children need now. Children need rich reading experiences from the very beginning, not after they've mastered a set of skills or reached a certain grade. And here's the thing: children, just as they are, are already capable of every aspect of a full reading life. So instead of thinking that this kind of work can only *happen if*, let's consider the reality that it can happen *even if*.

❦ *Even if* they can't yet read all of the text, children can listen to someone read to them, provided the person reading does so in an engaging, focused, positive way.

❦ *Even if* they've never talked about a text before or don't have much background knowledge on a topic or texts, children can respond to the ideas in a text by choosing something to notice and wonder about.

So when we plan what kinds of reading experiences children will have, let's consider that read-aloud offers all children opportunities to think deeply about a text, *even if.* And what happens if we apply that to ourselves? Even if we've never considered ourselves particularly insightful readers, we can offer children rich reading experiences, starting today! These experiences don't need to be perfect to be worthy of children's time. I think sometimes we're afraid to try because we have a vague notion of what it means to be perfect, and we don't believe we're quite there yet; we don't yet have a clear vision of how children can show their learning beyond test scores and ever-increasing text levels. Because we're not sure about what to look for, we can overlook the brilliance that's happening right in front of us.

Expecting Brilliance

One of the great joys of teaching is anticipating children's brilliance. When I walk into classrooms to work with children and teachers, it's always on my mind—how will this group of children surprise us today? And even though many of our thoughts are just processing, I know that when we pay attention to children and give them space, time, and support to think deeply, we can expect brilliance. And still, when it happens—that independent synthesis a child does, the bigness of the idea and the clarity of understanding about the world . . . well, the beauty of that thought and the pleasure of watching the child form it take my breath away.

It's moments like these that cause us to pause, just for a second or two, and think, "Wow. Did I just hear that?" Sometimes we're stunned—the child has said something in such a way that we don't quite believe what we're hearing—it's something we wish we'd thought to say.

I believe there are more moments of brilliance out there than we think. In the classroom our bodies, hearts, and minds move so quickly from one thing, one thought, one moment to the next that we aren't able to hear the beautiful thoughts and ideas that are all around us—children's and our own. So when we do happen to be in the right place at the right time, we might assume it's an anomaly.

I wonder what would happen if the unexpected became the expected?

What if we had the expectation that *children will be brilliant* on our radar, and we took specific action to slow down, listen with all of our being, and open our hearts and minds to the possibility of brilliance within every child in our care?

Many children don't yet know how to recognize or even what to do with a beautiful thought or idea—they might not even believe they're the kind of kids who have the capacity to think in these ways. They might think that everything they do is because of someone else, and they don't yet have an awareness of their own independent thinking, or their ability to choose a path to action. Or maybe children know they have beautiful thoughts but they don't know how to hold onto them or do something wonderful with all that great thinking. Our job is to show them that their thinking is worth holding onto. They need scaffolding and noticing for that beautiful independent thinking to happen and to learn what they can do with it.

I believe that read-aloud—the experience of sharing, noticing, thinking, and reflecting on a great text—can answer this need. It works because we're inviting children to pay attention to something—a book we've chosen because we're pretty sure children will love it and will be able to connect with it in some way. We're going for books that offer more sophisticated ideas than those they might choose or be able to read on their own; we understand the importance of listening comprehension, where big ideas and big thinking can flourish freely no matter where children are on the reading continuum.

During read-aloud, we're not telling children what to think; we're asking them what *they* think and feel. Children's independent thinking can be fostered in lots of different ways, of course, but because we're teaching reading, we make the focus a book; we're helping establish a behavior of thinking that goes beyond what they already know and helping them learn to construct meaning in a sincere, natural, no-pressure kind of way. Here's what I've figured out about how read-aloud can foster children's independent thinking.

How to Use Read-Aloud to Foster Independent Thinking

- Set a fixed daily time for read-aloud when all children will be present—no pullouts, please!

- Choose books that can be read aloud in one sitting and are interesting enough to read, think, and talk about more than once. These books don't have to connect to the curriculum in any way! You might have an eye toward that, but generally you're just choosing great books that you and your children can dig into, figure out, and love. We don't always have to have deep conversations during read-alouds; some of them are just plain fun. As always, think balance.

- The first time, read for joy! You might do some thinking aloud along the way, but keep it simple. Focus on what creates uncertainty. This is about authentic, in-the-moment thinking and modeling that shows what you do when you read and why.

The three actions above will make a big difference in your children's literacy and love of reading all on their own. If you want to do even more to foster independent thinking and actions, consider the ideas below.

- Invite children to also think aloud during portions of your read-aloud. Focus these conversations with a question that requires children to grapple with ideas and doesn't have one right answer. It's the uncertainty, the grappling together, that matters most.

- Listen in and observe these conversations; notice and name for yourself what you see and hear. If you can, jot your learning in a small notebook to use later—your notes just might help you plan for upcoming lessons, small-group work, and conferences.

- Notice the great thinking children have been doing and ask them what they would like to do with it.

Bring your read-aloud into readers' workshop:

- At the end of the daily read-aloud, hand the book off to a child. Ask, "Who would like to do some more thinking about this book during readers' workshop?"

- Use portions of the texts you've read aloud for explicit teaching during your minilessons the same day and in the days and weeks to come—how can you help children put to use what they know about the text already to dig deeper and use it as the foundation for discovering new learning?

- Apply what you've learned from listening in to read-aloud conversations to help you think through work time and minilessons.

- The read-aloud is a scaffold for children's independent thinking. During work time, children practice what they've learned about reading and thinking during read-aloud and transfer it to their independent reading. They've heard a proficient reader think aloud (that's you!) and they've had practice thinking aloud about big ideas with a partner— all this thinking has been made visible and accessible. Now they know how and why readers think and read at the same time.

And finally, **What might children create that's relevant to them and will help them hold onto their independent thinking and learning?**

- This works best when children have many choices about what this is and how it will look. This isn't about giving them three choices; it's about them deciding, "What do I want to make that will help me remember these big ideas I'm thinking about?" What they decide is highly personal and comes from within them—it's *their* way of creating an artifact that they can develop into something relevant for their lives.

Once they've experienced thinking in this way, once they understand how it feels, they'll become hooked on going below the surface; they'll want to delve in and do it again and again. It's fun to think about big ideas and create theories, and during read-aloud, they come to understand it's something they can do all on their own and with each other. They learn to honor and be proud of their individual and collective brilliance.

As teachers who understand that reading is a tool and a process, we remind ourselves that the means reflect the end. If we don't foster children's independence as readers, thinkers, and learners throughout all of children's learning about reading, they become dependent on our thinking and disengage from their own.

We recognize children's independent thinking by being present and paying attention to what they read, write, and talk about. We work to recognize full-on independence and glimmers of independence, too. Every step forward, be it big or be it small, matters. When we're present, we stand back and observe, listen in to children talking with partners and in small groups, and most of all, when we confer, listen more than we talk. We think of children's growing independence individually and collectively, asking questions like these to help us recognize brilliance and make decisions about who needs what and why:

Questions to Help Us Assess Children's Growth and Independence

What am I noticing about what children are **reading**?

- Are some of their book selections more sophisticated now than they were before?

- Are they interested in reading the books I've read aloud during independent work time?

- Do they take books from school to read at home or bring books from home to read at school?

- Do they ask for specific titles of books or books by a certain author?

What am I noticing about children's **talk**?

- Are they moving away from literal conversations and moving toward more inferential ones? Are conversations focused mostly on retelling, **or** are they asking questions, thinking about big ideas, making connections, and working to synthesize information?

- Do they talk with each other about books and authors they love all on their own?

- Do they form small, informal book clubs independently, where two or three children choose a book, or books, to read and talk about together? (Maybe it's a picture book, a collection of nonfiction books about a topic, a short chapter book, poetry, a wordless book, a graphic novel, an article . . . you name it.)

What am I noticing about what children **write** about our read-aloud texts?

- Do they have a pencil, sticky notes, and their notebook handy, just in case they need them?

- When I look closely at their work, what strikes me? Do I notice new ways of presenting or formatting information? Have they made their thinking visible? Could others learn from what they did?

- Can they explain why their work matters and consider what they might do with their thinking?

Of course we'll answer "not yet" to some of these questions, but now we have ideas of ways to move forward, either for the class as a whole or for individual children. It might mean doing more minilessons (or conferences, or both) about book selection, and recommendations, giving children more opportunities to talk about big ideas during read-aloud, allowing them more freedom in expressing themselves as they read. Choose an area of need—reading and book selection, talking about ideas, or more time for written or artistic response. They're all connected—focusing on one area (reading, writing, or talking) will naturally lend itself to new understandings of the other two.

Please, No Pullouts

Some say that all children are capable but then make exceptions. Either you believe it's true—and it *is* true—or you don't. I see this when I do demonstration lessons in classrooms. Every now and again, a teacher will tell me that at certain times during the workshop there will be children coming and going for a variety of reasons—this day, Adeline and Rene will be leaving for reading intervention, Maija has speech class, and John won't be joining us because he might be disruptive and the work we're doing will be too hard for him.

I'm all about children receiving the help they need. But when do they receive it, and at what cost? I nearly swooned when I heard Dick Allington say at a conference, "Reading intervention should be in addition to readers' workshop, not instead of it." I'd say the same is true for read-alouds.

John was one of those students frequently pulled out during readers' workshop. I convinced his teacher to let him stay with us for some demonstration teaching through read-aloud, because unless it's absolutely necessary, I really don't want any child to be removed from class on my account. (This is supposed to be an authentic teaching and learning experience for everyone!) And here's what I know to be true: the children teachers worry about and consider removing during my visit almost always prove that they're capable and successful during our time together. But this isn't because of me. Things go well most of the time because I have no preconceived notions about any of the children sitting before me—in my eyes, they are all capable.

I know that's easy to say—I'm there only a few days, and there's some novelty in having another teacher as well as lots of observers in the classroom. But still, experiences like these show that our preconceived notions can harm children and deny them the learning experiences they so desperately need and deserve.

So it was with John.

The previous day I'd read aloud *Wolfsnail: A Backyard Predator*, by Sarah Campbell. Children had been working on strategies for remembering what they'd learned in informational texts, and on this day, I asked them what they remembered about wolfsnails from our read-aloud the day before.

John raised his hand. "Come on up, John," I said. "What do you remember?"

He came up front, and then he froze. I told the class that John was the kind of kid who knew that thinking and remembering take time and we were going to give him all the time he needed. We waited, and he said, "They live in a shell. They have a slimy foot that helps them move. They eat snails and slugs, and they follow their slime to find them."

A child asked me, "How did John remember all that?"

I replied, "You should ask John."

John explained he remembered most of what I'd read *and* he had the pictures from the book in his mind. He took the book from my hands and showed us the picture of the wolfsnail inside a shell and one of the slimy foot, and he pointed to something he thought was a slime trail.

"Wow, John," I said. "Do you do this a lot as a reader and a thinker?" (I was elevating him in his eyes and everyone else's too—John was a reader and a thinker. And when someone else sees you as that kind of kid, you just might begin to think it's true.) "Is it like you have a camera in your head? You take photos in your mind of what you want to remember, and then you connect it to the words?"

He said, "Sort of like that."

"Would it be OK with you if some kids decide to try out your strategy today? Should we call it John's strategy?" He thought we should. Children who wanted to learn more about this strategy stayed up front; the rest shifted to independent reading. John helped us sort it out a little more, and I recorded what he said on chart paper for everyone to see:

John's Strategy for Remembering and Understanding Informational Text

❖ Look at the pictures for a while; try to notice everything and hold it in your mind.

❖ Read all the words you can.

❖ Go back to the picture and put what you know from the words with it.

Thanks for teaching us, John!

What's significant here? Let's imagine John in this moment. He's not a child with special needs right now. He's John. It's normal for labels to cloud our vision of a child, but too often labels get in the way of how we view children; we make false assumptions and expect less. So we must use structures that allow for student success. Read-aloud can help us do that.

We want to be mindful of when children are pulled out of class for special services. Maybe we think the read-aloud isn't important, in light of all the child's instructional needs. But I'd argue read-aloud is exactly what this child, and every child, needs. Instead of thinking about what a specific child can't do, we offer them all the real experience that we want for them and then figure out the scaffolds they need to get them there. Too often, children like John don't get the immersive reading experiences that help readers grow. But in a read-aloud, everyone takes on the identity of a reader.

And some, like John, take on the identity of a teacher, too.

▓ Finding Time for Read-Aloud

Let's go back to those teachers who observed Val's first graders. They spent much of the afternoon working together in small groups, envisioning learning situations similar to what they'd seen and considering what they needed to make it work. As I listened in to hear them talk about what they saw, I heard them talk about the power of read-aloud, specifically how the children they'd just observed were able to identify big ideas in stories because they'd heard and talked about them before. Many became wistful, thinking back to when read-aloud was an everyday occurrence—a time when children gathered together, leaned in or sat back, opened their eyes wide (or closed them), and listened to their teacher read aloud.

They aren't alone. This wistfulness for read-aloud is widespread. When I ask, "What happened to read-aloud?" the number one answer is, "We don't have time." With prescribed units, minute-by-minute teaching and learning formats, narrowing curricula, and high-stakes testing requirements, read-aloud for many teachers has been relegated to "when I can fit it in." But I know (and research supports this conclusion) that read-aloud, when combined with think-aloud, student talk, and practice in real books, accomplishes these things and more, in deeper and more authentic and relevant ways. Just think about those first graders from the beginning of this chapter!

Teachers get wistful about read-aloud because they remember it as a special time, a coming together during the day when children could listen, think, talk, and grow. It should be daily, shared experience that levels the playing field—everyone can be brilliant here, and everyone knows it! Read-aloud elevates us all—we often feel inspired afterward, vowing to be our kinder, braver, better selves. And just to be clear, this coming together for read-aloud isn't only for workshop classrooms. Read-aloud is for every classroom, every child, every teacher, every day.

Val reads aloud to her first graders every day. At three o'clock, she plays the song of the week on her classroom computer, and children know to clean up their work spaces, get their stuff packed up for home, and join Val in the meeting area for read-aloud. The packing up feels a little chaotic, but when children make their way to the carpet and find a seat, things change. They settle. There's a feeling of anticipation, happiness, and that certain kind of calm that comes over kids when we read aloud.

Val understands read-aloud is for everyone. That's why she places it at the end of the day when there are no pullouts and very few interruptions. This is when she and her students strengthen their relationships with each other, bolster literate classroom communities, forge identities, and become deeper thinkers and thoughtful people.

Val keeps a stack of books at the ready; there's no grabbing just any book off the shelf. When she chooses books for read-aloud, she asks herself, "Will this book give the children and me something to think and talk about? Does it offer a variety of perspectives? Is it engaging, relevant, and worthy of our time?"

Val doesn't wait until everyone is seated and ready to begin reading. She begins at three o'clock on the dot, and it takes only a day or two at the beginning of the year before children are ready and waiting at that time. She reads aloud picture books, at least one a day, every day. Chapter books used to be her go-to for read-aloud, but now she believes shorter texts offer her children more depth and variety in their reading experiences—they can listen to fifteen picture books in three weeks rather than just one chapter book.

What the Research Tells Us

Reading aloud to students is a consistently recommended practice for elementary language arts to promote students' understanding and engagement with text (Dugan, 1997; Sipe, 2000-2002), motivation to read (Morrow, 2003; Palmer, Codling, and Gambrell, 1994), and development of reading processes (Fisher, Flood, Lapp, and Frey, 2004). The National Research Council (Snow et al., 1998) recommended the use of read-aloud, "The single most important activity for building the knowledge required for eventual success in reading . . ." (Gabriel, 23)

Wow, right?

In light of this research (and the realization of what children were missing), teachers I've worked with challenged themselves to look closely at their schedules to find fifteen or so minutes somewhere in the day that they could consistently dedicate to read-aloud. They looked at everything students did from the time they walked in the door to the final bell. Did they find the minutes they needed? They did! Here are some of the practices teachers eliminated, shortened, or combined in the name of read-aloud:

❖ *The "top of the morning" worksheets:* Eliminated. Fifteen minutes gained.

❖ *Morning jobs*: Shortened from thirty minutes to fifteen or twenty. Ten to fifteen minutes gained.

❖ *Calendar work*: Shortened from twenty minutes to ten. Ten minutes gained.

❖ *Whole-class bathroom breaks*: Eliminated. Replaced with a system for children to use the bathroom as needed. Almost twenty to thirty minutes gained in classes where there were previously two breaks a day.

❖ *Snack time*: Combined with morning or afternoon recess. Ten minutes gained.

Remember: The read-aloud can happen anytime during the school day. It's not *when* you do it in a day, but *that* you do it every day!

▒ Reading Aloud for Joy

I encourage teachers to do read-aloud outside readers' workshop. Outside of workshop is when you read aloud an entire picture book for the joy of it. Then, when it's time for workshop, you won't need to read the entire book—you'll have done that already! Now you can focus on just a few pages—those that will best allow you to think aloud and focus your attention on your teaching point or learning target. And you won't have given up the benefits and joys that read-aloud brings you and your students.

When introducing a book, there's no need to tell children all about the story or spend a lot of time building background knowledge. Think about it— would you engage in a story if you already knew what was going to happen? That takes the thinking and the joy of story away!

I try to read a book on my own first before reading it aloud to children; there aren't many of us who can do a great read-aloud cold. I want to know where it makes sense to pause, when to raise my voice, and when to lower it. There's a bit of drama in the read-aloud—not a full-on production, but for sure a thoughtful, nuanced read. I'm hoping children will savor the story, the words, and the time we spend together in this way. I read ahead with my eyes when I'm reading aloud; this way I'm just a few steps ahead of the words and don't have

to look at the book the whole time—on these occasions I can look children in the face, drawing them in with my eyes and facial expressions. (We're in this together!) I often get out of my chair and move closer, reading aloud crouched down on my knees, sharing in the intimacy of the experience.

We've talked about how read-alouds can be interactive, but they don't always have to be. There is also something deeply satisfying about listening to a great book and letting the words wash over you with no demands. Communities grow through talk, but not exclusively. Sometimes being part of a shared experience is all we need to grow. And besides, we know we'll have other opportunities to dig deeper into this book on another day; it doesn't need to be our priority now.

Reading aloud for joy also means reading a variety of genres—you want children to see how many choices they have and how many diverse texts they can delight in!

It took me some time to feel at home and find my way when reading aloud nonfiction. Books that helped me bridge the gap between reading aloud fiction and nonfiction are books like these: *One Tiny Turtle* and *Bat Loves the*

Night, by Nicola Davies; *Wolfsnail: A Backyard Predator* and *Mysterious Patterns*, by Sarah Campbell; *Butterfly Eyes* and *Swirl by Swirl*, by Joyce Sidman; *Animals Nobody Loves*, by Seymour Simon; and *Shark Lady* and *Pink Is for Blobfish*, by Jess Keating.

When I read aloud to a group of children nowadays, teachers are always watching *me*. But I really wish they weren't. The truth is, I have the best seat in the house—I get to watch children's faces and the range of emotions read-aloud brings. I see scrunched-up faces, smiling faces, curious, surprised, and giggling faces. I see indignant faces, mad faces, and sometimes teary, sad faces. Sometimes all in one read-aloud!

And when children talk about a book in twos and threes, we all get to listen in on the brilliance in their words, see the animation in their faces, and witness the joy read-aloud brings. Children give me energy when I read aloud, and I give them my energy in return. The joy is reciprocated. Just like the clown fish and the sea anemone, we have a mutually beneficial, beautiful symbiotic relationship!

Read-aloud lifts all of us up, and honestly, on some days it lifts me up the most. Just looking out at them in this brief moment in time reminds me why my work, our work, matters.

We share the magic of a great book.

▓▓ Teachers and Children Thinking Aloud

While read-aloud is important all on its own, there are a few simple things teachers can do to maximize children's experiences and foster independent thinking. We can:

❖ think aloud as we read;

❖ invite children to think aloud during whole-group and partner discussions;

❖ invite children to "step into the story";

❖ listen in to what they say; and

❖ put the books we read aloud into the hands of kids.

What the Research Tells Us

One of the things they are learning [from us] is what thinking looks like. In thoughtful classrooms, a disposition toward thinking is always on display. Teachers show their curiosity and interest. They display open-mindedness and the willingness to consider alternative perspectives. Teachers model their own process of seeking truth and understanding. They show a healthy skepticism and demonstrate what it looks like to be strategic in one's thinking. They frequently put their own thinking on display and model what it means to be reflective. This demonstration of thinking sets the tone for the classroom, establishing both the expectations for thought and fostering students' inclination toward thinking. (Ritchhart 2002, 161)

Thinking Aloud as We Read

Thinking aloud during read-aloud time is different from thinking aloud during a minilesson. When we think aloud during read-aloud, we're revealing what readers think about, but we're not being specific or asking children what they notice us doing, or naming it for them. We're just being ourselves as readers during the natural course of reading. At the same time, we're also modeling reading behaviors, so during a read-aloud, I might go back to reread a section to confirm my thinking; ask questions; look closely at pictures; make predictions; laugh when something is funny; think about big ideas; or simply mark with a sticky note a page I want to go back to later. The vibe during read-aloud is natural, authentic, and joyful—it's a reader being a reader.

I'm after authentic literary moments for children, yes, but for myself too. (For example, after reading Dan Santat's *After the Fall*, I found myself thinking aloud, "What? Humpty Dumpty is a *bird*?" A child told me, "Well, birds come from eggs, you know, and turn the page back—see how he's growing some feathers? It's a *clue*." Ah. I hadn't noticed that!)

We'll have plenty of other opportunities for more explicit instruction during minilessons, individual conferences, and small-group work. In these situations, we're teaching children something specific, thinking with them about why it matters, and showing them how we go about doing it. I often use the books from read-alouds to help me teach my minilessons. For example, say I'm teaching children about the importance of merging what they've learned from the pictures and the words—I can refer back to *After the Fall* to make my point:

"Remember last month when we read this book, and Isla noticed the feathers sprouting on Humpty Dumpty on this page here? She was paying close attention to the words and the pictures, right? I hadn't looked closely enough, so I was really surprised. . . ."

During this minilesson, I don't have to reread *After the Fall* in its entirety—children have heard it several times before and they have a schema for the story and how it goes.

The vibe for thinking aloud during the minilesson is also natural, authentic, and joyful—it's all about purpose. Think-alouds during read-aloud are more implicit (this is what readers do); think-alouds during minilessons are more explicit (this is why and how readers do it).

Inviting Children to Think Aloud

Invite children to think aloud during discussions in the whole group, and especially with a partner during read-aloud. This is significant: Thinking aloud with a group or another person about a compelling question, problem, or idea, particularly when someone else is reading it aloud, gives children opportunities to think together, wrestle with ideas, puzzle things through, and cocreate meaning in ways that the books they can read on their own don't always allow. These are powerful and necessary conversations—children are digging deep to make their thinking visible for themselves and each other in ways that some have never been exposed to or realized they were capable of. It's a heady experience and one we want them to be comfortable having with friends and on their own.

Inviting Children into the Story

I also love inviting children to "step into the story" during a read-aloud. I ask them to become a specific character and actually speak for him or her—"What is this character thinking about right now? What is he or she wrestling with?" For example, I'm reading aloud Cynthia Rylant's *An Angel for Solomon Singer*, and we're on the page where he's standing on the streets of New York City, and things have begun to get better for him; his views of the world have changed since we met him at the beginning of the book. I say, "Is there someone who would feel comfortable stepping into the story and becoming Solomon Singer? Look at his face—see how his expression is different now than it was in the beginning? Who wants to become Solomon Singer and explain how he's feeling in this place and time?" When a child volunteers, I ask her to look closely at the picture in the book and get into character—put her hands in her pockets and look up at the sky like Solomon and speak for him. And then she becomes that character, right before our eyes. (We've had many, many visitors over the years . . . Oliver Button *and* the boys who bullied him, Amazing Grace, Gerald and Piggie, the bad seed, Maya, Chloe, Humpty Dumpty, and Eugenie Clark, to name a few.)

I'm intentional about what I ask children to think about—I decide with kids in mind, and I also consider my uncertainties (what don't I get?). When I'm working to figure something out, there's a good chance children are too. For an example, let's go back to *After the Fall*. There's a page close to the beginning of the book where Humpty Dumpty is lying all in a puddle on the floor, a blanket covering him, his eyes somehow distant and haunting. The words let us know that even though he was mostly put back together again at the King's County Hospital, they weren't able to fix all of him. So I say during a read-aloud, "Look closely at the picture and listen to the words again. What does this make you think about? Share your ideas with someone sitting close to you." (Or I could say, "Look closely at Humpty in this picture. What's going on? Who wants to step into the story and speak for him?")

I'm convinced that thinking aloud with a partner (and stepping into the story) is an important scaffold for independent thinking—it's precisely the same kind of talk, the same kind of conversation, we want children to have inside their heads when they're out on their own, reading independently.

Listening in to What They Say

When children are talking, I'm up and out of my chair, listening to what they're saying, noticing and naming (inside my head) what I'm hearing, and sometimes jotting it in a small notebook. I'm focusing on questions like these: Who is going beyond the text and previous discussions and thinking in new ways, taking on the work of independent thinking? What's the gist of what they're saying? Whose talk closely mirrors what has already been said? Who seems at a loss for words or unengaged? I'll use this information to help me plan minilessons, small-group work, and individual conferences during upcoming workshops—it's yet another way for me to understand where kids are now and what they need in order to move forward. And I remind myself to listen *to* what the child has to say, rather than *for* a certain kind of thinking. This is all about understanding where the child is now (listening to) rather than where I want him or her to be (listening for).

"So are you ready to step into the story? Start with I . . ."

Handing Read-Alouds off to Kids

Sometimes we think the books we read aloud are only for us, and we keep them on a special shelf, way up high. But what if we put these books in the hands of children instead? What if, at the end of read-aloud, we said, "So who would like to do some more thinking with this book?" We could then give it to any child who wanted it, knowing that reading level wouldn't matter—this would be about thinking, and the student would have already heard it. The child would be able to dig deeper into the book now, picking up where we left off, thinking about new ideas and creating yet another layer of meaning for himself, all by himself.

What's the Best That Could Happen? Being Inspired to Act

We do read-aloud for the value of that experience alone, but our hope is that children will generate such great thinking that they'll believe they should do more with it. When we invite children to do something with their thinking, we send the message that their thinking matters, that it has value and so do they. When we send out invitations across grades and over time, what they decide to do has the potential to shape who they are, what they believe, and how they view the world and their place in it. Children come to understand their thinking, and their voices are powerful, and they have the capacity, and sometimes the responsibility, to influence others.

In the examples that follow, you'll see a few ways this might look, in kindergarten through grade four. Some examples show children doing something with their thinking across a whole class, some with a partner or in a small group, and still others independently. Read-aloud is prominent in all these classrooms, along with teacher and student think-alouds, reading, writing, talking, and independent practice. (But you knew that!)

Emily Finney's first graders were in an informational unit and wanted to do a play to inform others about endangered animals. They chose animals they wanted to highlight and made masks. They wrote scripts, glued them on the back of the masks for easy reading, and then took their show (and pleas) on the road. (Actually, down the hall.)

Children wrote a play to inspire others to act on behalf of endangered animals. They wore these necklaces around their necks with the script on back.

Tera

Giant Panda are being hunted. There are only 2,000 pandas left. Nice people are helping these animals but they are still endangered!

I am no longer endangered. This is what will happen if you help these animals.

Children in Susan Phillips' and Amy Brock's classrooms were inspired by fictional characters and real people in picture books Susan and Amy read aloud. Children each chose and spent time with one book that spoke to them, ultimately creating posters (and more!) and hanging them in and around their school's entranceway and library in order to inspire others to read their book and take action, too.

My name is Lila Be. After I read the book <u>One smile</u>. It inspired me to share my kindness to everyone. If we are nice to everyone they will be nice to me and you. That's why you should not be a bully or be rude.

If you don't understand what being nice means. It means to wait for your turn in line instead of cutting in line. It also means not to steal something from someone else. It means to have some kindness to everyone even to the people you hate.

Always have one smile on your face. If you are kind to others and help others someday they could help you in return.

Hi my name is Andrea Pinela. After I read the book <u>One Plastic Bag</u>, I was inspired to pick up bags and be createful and make something out of it. I wanted to do this because I want our city to be nice and clean. I do not want our city to be dirty.

I feel frustrated that there is trash along the streets. I made purses and wallets out of old bags and Caprison packages. I recyled these items so they won't land up on the ground. You should try recyling your trash too. What creative things can you make?

Through read-alouds and independent reading, children chose characters and public figures that inspired them!

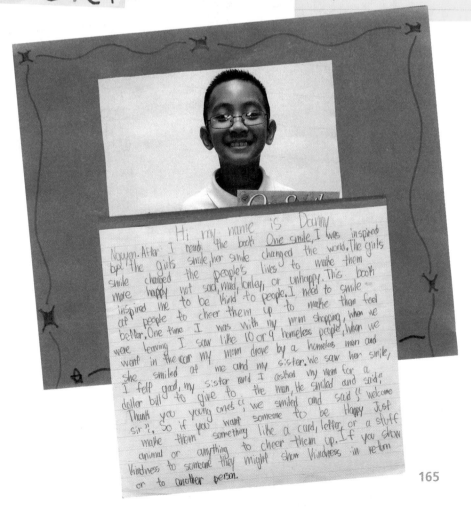

Hi my name is Danny Nguyen. After I read the book <u>One smile</u>, I was inspired by. The girls smile, her smile changed the world. The girls smile changed the people's lives to make them more happy not sad, mad, lonley, or unhappy. This book inspired me to be kind to people. I need to smile at people to cheer them up to make them feel better. One time I was with my mom shopping, when we were leaving I saw like 10 or 9 homeless people, when we went in the car my mom drove by a homeless man and she smiled at me and my sister. We saw her smile, I felt good, my sister and I asked my mom for a dollar bill to give to the man, He smiled and said "Thank you young ones" we smiled and said " welcome sir", so if you want someone to be Happy Just make them something like a card, letter, or a stuffe animal or anything to cheer them up. If you show Kindness to someone they might show Kindness in return or to another person.

And the children in Megan Burns' kindergarten went full-on public service, thinking of a myriad of ways they could make a difference in the world. Megan did lots of read-alouds, she handed the books off to kids, and they read and worked together in pairs and individually to think about what they could do with all their thinking.

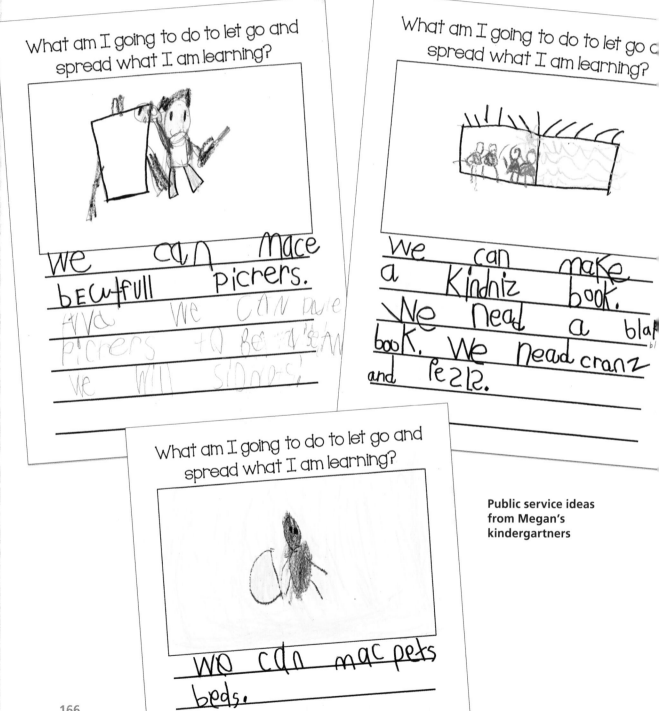

Public service ideas from Megan's kindergartners

Alexander making muffins for a homeless shelter, inspired by the wordless book *A Circle of Friends*

Photos by Megan Burns

Robert planting flowers outside the school, inspired by the book *Plant a Kiss*

Alijah making bird feeders, inspired by *How to Heal a Broken Wing*

Child working on a whole-class blanket for a homeless shelter, inspired by *A Circle of Friends*

Children planting a tree, inspired by *Little Tree*

These children were invited to do something with their thinking about reading and it showed in gorgeous, brilliant ways. As children have more practice doing something important with their thinking, it becomes a natural part of what they do as readers—they read, write, and talk about books, knowing that books have the power to inform, challenge, and change who we are and how we view the world. And knowing that they have the power, and sometimes even the responsibility, to give back—to inform, synthesize, challenge, and even change the way others view the world.

When children consistently do something important with their thinking, they read differently. They read to understand and learn, and they read with a bigger purpose—they believe they have an *obligation*, to themselves and others, to synthesize their learning.

In Emily Callahan's fourth-grade class, children routinely do something with their thinking. Take a look at Aisatu's "Endangered" piece, an open letter to wild animal hunters.

Aisatu's letter to hunters

It's edgy, and Aisatu means it to be—she wants her voice to be heard, acted upon, and remembered. Imagine being ten and believing your work, your voice, matters. How must that feel? Where might it lead? We're growing readers and citizens of the world here, day by day by day.

Mery and Makenzie were inspired by Emily's read-aloud of *Wangari's Trees of Peace*, by Jeannette Winter. The two gathered as many books about Wangari Maathai as they could, raiding classroom, school, and public libraries.

I Am Wangari
By: Mercy Toma & Makenzie Talbot

I walk with pride
Down the long hill
And to the stream
And watch the squirming tadpoles
But my mom always complained
I spent too much time in the world
Of nature

Goodbye all!
I'll miss you
I'm going to America
To figure out
Who I'm supposed to be
Through education

But when I returned
My village
It's empty
The fields that were green
Have now disappeared
I can't believe my eyes

I'm frustrated
I need to do something
Wildlife
Green nature
It's all gone
It's a struggle
Just to get water
They're suffering
And I need to do
Something
I need to plant trees
I speak out to my people
"The earth is naked.
For me the mission was
To try and cover it
with green"

I gather people
Women
Kids
Men
Grandmothers
Grandfathers
To help me with
Find a solution
To this crisis
For Kenya
Shall not suffer
Anymore

Along the way
I suffered consequences
Let me tell you the story
Soldiers came to me
They beat me
On my head
With metal bars
There were many
One put handcuffs on me
They thought this would
Stop me from planting
But no

Now I'm a doctor
I'm a mother of two
And a beloved wife
I won the green belt movement
I was the first
African woman
To receive
The Nobel Peace Prize
I made Kenya green
I'm all that my mother
Wanted me to be

R.I.P. Dr. Wangari Maathai
Dedicated to such an African woman that accomplished her dream to make the world a better place

Photos by Emily Callahan

Mercy and Makenzie's process work and poem

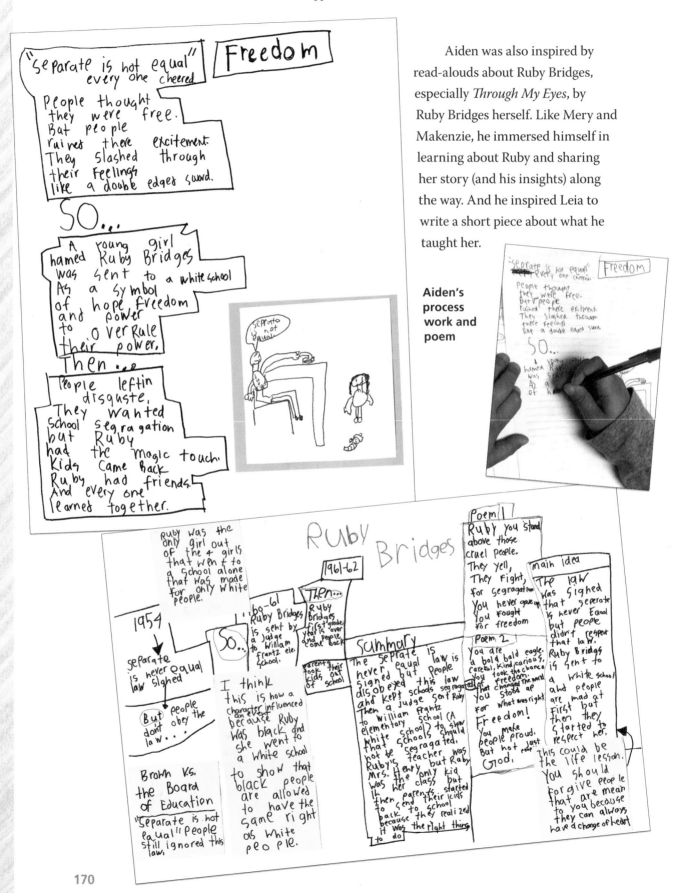

"Separate is not equal" every one cheered.

Freedom

People thought they were free. But people ruined there excitement. They slashed through their feelings like a double edged sword.

So...

A young girl named Ruby Bridges was sent to a white school As a symbol of hope freedom and power to over rule their power.

Then...

People left in disguste. They wanted school segragation but Ruby had the magic touch. Kids came back Ruby had friends. And every one learned together.

Aiden was also inspired by read-alouds about Ruby Bridges, especially *Through My Eyes*, by Ruby Bridges herself. Like Mery and Makenzie, he immersed himself in learning about Ruby and sharing her story (and his insights) along the way. And he inspired Leia to write a short piece about what he taught her.

Aiden's process work and poem

Ruby was the only girl out of the 4 girls that went to a school alone that was made for only white people.

Ruby Bridges

1961-62

Then...

Ruby Bridges first grade year is over and people come back

1954

separate is never equal law sighed

1960-61 Ruby Bridges is sent by a judge to William Frantz ele. school.

But people don't obey the law....

parents took their kids out of school

Brown V.S. the Board of Education "Separate is not equal" people still ignored this law.

I think this is how a character influenced an event because Ruby was black and she went to a white school to show that black people are allowed to have the same right as white people.

Summary The separate is never equal law is signed but people disobeyed this law and kept schools segragated. Then a judge sent Ruby to William frantz elementary school (A white school) to show that white schools shauld not be segragated. Ruby's teacher was Mrs. Henry but Ruby was the only kid in her class but then parents started to send their kids back to school because they realized it was the right thing to do

Poem 1 Ruby you stand above those cruel people. They yell, They fight, for segragation You never gave up You fought for freedom

Poem 2 You are a bold bald eagle. Careful, kind curious, You took the chance that changed the world You stood up for what was right Freedom! You make people proud. But not just people. God.

main idea The law was sighed that seperate is never Equal but people didn't respect that law. Ruby Bridges is sent to a white school and people are mad at first but then they started to respect her.

this could be the life lesson. You should forgive people that are mean to you because they can always have a change of heart

Do Aisatu, Mery, Makenzie, Aiden, Leia, and all the children showcased have more to learn about these topics and themselves? Of course they do! But they're opening doors that need to be opened, thinking about things they need to be thinking about, and doing things they need to be doing. All because of read-aloud! When we create conditions like those I've talked about here, we nurture thoughtful, reflective, impassioned human beings, the kind of people who know who they are, what they believe, and how they might make a difference in the lives of those around them and beyond.

If we're not teaching children to be independent thinkers, what are we teaching them? Compliance. Surely they deserve more than doing what we do, thinking as we think, answering questions we ask. Reading aloud and talking broaden our horizons—they allow children and teachers to question a text, think about big ideas, and learn from each other, understanding that we are all part of a bigger whole. And just think—children can be on their way with just fifteen minutes a day!

As they threaten... You walk like water c̄ oil separated

As they threaten... You walk peacefully

As they threaten... You say no more

As they threaten... You are already in the school you were transfered to.

As they threaten... You pray

Aiden Gabert and I were reading about Ruby Brigdes And Aiden wrote a poem and that inspired me!

And this is the poem I wrote inspired by Aiden Gabert!

Leia's response to Aiden

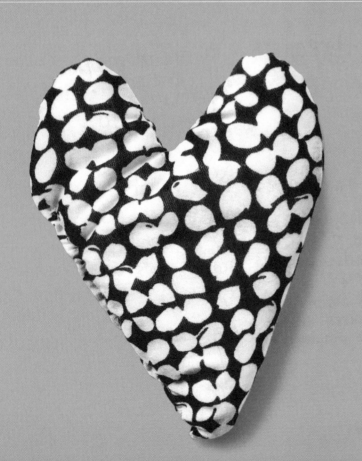

Things that may never be an actual part of our teaching are parts of us and thus affect everything we touch. Who we are is woven into how we behave, how we approach colleagues, how we envision our work, our world, and our future together. We need to take the time, no matter how hectic our days become, to stare out at the sea or to sit quietly in the yard or up on the rooftop and ask ourselves what it is we care about and how honestly we share our lives and passions with one another and our students. New methods of instruction will continue to evolve in direct proportion to who we are, and how much of that we are willing to bring to our teaching.

(BARBIERI)

Conclusion

IN PURSUIT OF BEAUTIFUL QUESTIONS

This is the crux of it, isn't it? What we care about, who we are, and how much of that we are willing to bring to our teaching? I've kept this quote in my notebook for years now because it's a reminder to stay real, to be true to myself, and to be the same person inside the classroom as I am in my life outside it. Because when there's a disconnect, when we act one way in the classroom and another way in the rest of our lives, we have to disengage from one part of ourselves to engage with the other, and that can be hard. When we don't feel like we can be ourselves, we lose the uniqueness of who we are, and our identities both inside and outside the classroom are diminished in ways we'll never quite know.

Sometimes I think this is because we have misconceptions about what it actually means to be a teacher. We might think we need to take on a different persona, that we have to be this way or that way, say this thing or that thing, be like this teacher or that teacher. None of this is true. Our first priority is to be our very best authentic selves, the best teachers and people we can be. Our next priority is the children we teach.

Just as we need to view children as capable, and on that basis imagine new possibilities, we have to view ourselves as capable, too. Asking a beautiful question frees us to look beyond the limitations of what we've done so far, and opens us up to new possibilities of what might be in our future, expanding how we perceive teaching and learning, allowing us to become more thoughtful and hopeful, agentive and alive.

And that is what this book is all about. It's about asking your own beautiful questions, trusting and believing in yourself, learning more about who you are, striving to be better. I think we all want that—to be better, to evolve, to see ourselves as the kind of teachers who are vulnerable enough to know there's always more to learn. It takes courage and commitment, this stepping back to reflect and question whether we're on the right path.

Dylan Wiliam once said, "If we create a culture where every teacher believes they need to improve, not because they aren't good enough, but because they can be even better, there's no limit to what we can achieve." I've shared the stories of so many teachers in this book because I wanted you to experience the culture Wiliam describes within these pages. I wish the larger culture gave this to teachers, but I think we have to acknowledge that we need to create this for ourselves. Pursuing beautiful questions like these on our own means we sit with some feelings that can be hard to embrace—uncertainty, mystery, and doubt. It can feel easier to abandon whatever it is that's making us feel this way and get on with things. But when we become comfortable with feeling uncomfortable by asking beautiful questions, we discover our truth in the process.

What can we look forward to? What motivates us to sit with discomfort and see where our beautiful questions lead us? Your classroom might have the feel of this one: Children were immersed in an author study of Chris Van Allsburg, working to understand him as an author and what he wanted for his readers. One of the overarching questions in this unit was, How would you introduce Chris Van Allsburg to someone who didn't know his work? (Just in case you're not familiar with him, his books are part fantasy, part reality. His stories are mysterious, leaving much to the imagination, and his illustrations are eerie, beautiful, and a little bit creepy. In other words, perfect for an author study!)

It was day two of this fifteen-day unit, and all twenty-seven students were poring over his books, talking, wondering, and thinking together in twos and threes. Jaclyn (their teacher) and I had planned to jump in and confer with them, but in the midst of it all, we looked at each other and decided to wait—we figured we just might learn more by standing back a bit, listening in, and noticing what we saw and heard.

It was a good call.

We noticed that children weren't looking for quick and easy answers to their questions; they seemed open to all possibilities, and nothing anyone said was considered off-limits. They were willing to suspend reality for now and accept things that felt surreal and strange. They savored the uncertainty, the mystery of Chris Van Allsburg and his books, seemingly relishing their doubts and fears. We heard Camran share his thinking about the book *The Stranger* with a friend. "Chris Van Allsburg is out there, you know? Like, who is the stranger, really? I don't even know yet, but all his books so far are heart-hitting."

His friend looked up. "Heart-hitting? What's that mean?"

Camran answered, "Heart-hitting is how the book makes you feel. The heart part is something very sad, or very happy, or even weird; it goes to your heart. Hitting is how it makes you feel." He emphasized his point by pounding his fist to his heart, saying, "Just like that: it hits you right there."

Conversations like this one were everywhere—children were curious about and captivated by Chris Van Allsburg and his books, happy in the moment, in the messiness of it all. And when it became time to transition to

writing workshop, they couldn't let go—they had more reading to do, theories to develop, questions to figure out.

This is exactly what Jaclyn had had in mind. She'd decided to let her noticing be her focus in these early days of this unit, not some busy form of doing. She was freeing children to do their own thinking in their own way, and she was freeing herself to listen and learn.

When I went back to my hotel that night, I thought about Jaclyn and her kids and wished all kids experiences like these. In Jaclyn's class, children:

* ❖ knew where they were headed;

* ❖ remained open to possibilities instead of limiting themselves;

* ❖ savored uncertainty and mystery and didn't let their doubts and fears paralyze them;

* ❖ accepted the messiness of learning, viewing it as joyful; and

* ❖ stayed curious, sticking with it.

I wish the same for teachers. Because the two go hand in hand, right? When teachers welcome curiosity, messiness, and mystery for themselves, most of their kids do too.

So what gets in our way? Sometimes I think we take ourselves too seriously. Not our teaching of course, but ourselves as teachers. We're afraid to let go, experiment, try out new ways of doing things because we think we don't have the freedom to do that, and therefore we don't have the capacity or don't want to expend the energy it takes to position ourselves anywhere outside the norm. But is this really true?

Remember this from Tom Newkirk? "If we are honest with ourselves, it is not always external forces that inhibit us. We all can be victims of our own inertia, when we feel passive and mediocre and tired—so that even the thought of making a change and investigating it feels like too much effort" (2016, 9).

There are steps to freedom.

We have to slow ourselves down and be metacognitive, to be aware of and think about our thinking in order to begin to free ourselves.

What can we do that others are doing for us?

If the primary obstacle to children's freedom is our own, then what can we do to remove this obstacle?

Asking beautiful questions is one way in, and we all have freedom in how we respond to questions of practice. Our freedom might be more limited at times than is ideal, but it's still there.

So, are you ready to get started? Asking your own beautiful questions begins by being honest with yourself, asking, "What about my teaching doesn't feel right?" Nothing is too small or too large to tackle; if something doesn't feel right, you've got a beautiful question just waiting to be asked. In this book, I've shared many examples of teachers taking something that felt off and turning it into a beautiful question that led them to better practice. There are more I could have shared, like these:

Teacher's Observation	Resulting Beautiful Question
"Kids are groaning about reading logs, they don't like writing summaries after they read a book, and annotating is getting old. But how else can I hold them accountable?" (Concerned about ways children are being asked to respond to reading)	What if children had choice in the ways they responded to their reading?
"Some days it feels like a waste of time, and kids get tired of hearing about everyone else's books." (Concerned about the direction of the class' reflection and share time)	What if reflection and share time focused on the reader, not on the reading?
"My intentions are good, and I know it's what kids need, but we always run out of time. I end up feeling guilty on the days we don't have it." (Concerned about not having free-choice independent reading)	What if the first twenty minutes of each day were dedicated to free-choice independent reading?

Observation chart

Once you know what you want to focus on, it's smart to let kids in on what you're working to figure out—you're honoring them in the process, and you're enlisting their help to make things better.

Dear Reader, Now that you've read this book, you're more than ready to come together with children, inviting them alongside you to move forward, to evolve, and to grow together. (You already were, but this book was written to convince you of that.) We find ways into each other's hearts, we make our voices heard, and we find the courage to set out and engage with the possibilities and promise each day brings. We ask and answer our beautiful questions.

(And if you need some more inspiration, read the picture books *All in a Day*, by Cynthia Rylant, and *The Way to Start a Day* and *I'm in Charge of Celebrations*, both by Byrd Baylor.)

Good luck. Best wishes. And I'd love to hear where this takes you!

–Debbie

Join the conversation about *What's the Best That Could Happen?*

at **www.facebook.com/groups/WhatsTheBest**.

References

Allyn, Pam. 2017. "Why Is the Read-Aloud a Life-Changing Form of Civic Learning?" *Literacy and NCTE* (blog), September 23. www2.ncte.org /blog/2017/09/read-aloud-life-changing-form-civic-learning/.

Bennett, Samantha. 2007. *That Workshop Book*: *New Systems and Structures for Classrooms That Read, Write, and Think*. Portsmouth, NH: Heinemann.

Berger, Warren. 2014. *A More Beautiful Question: The Power of Inquiry to Spark Breakthrough Ideas*. New York: Bloomsbury.

Boelts, Maribeth. 2007. *Those Shoes*. Somerville, MA: Candlewick.

Bransford, John D., Ann L. Brown, and Rodney R. Cocking, eds.. 2000. *How People Learn: Brain, Mind, Experience, and School*. Expanded edition. Washington, DC: National Academy Press.

Brown, Peter C., Henry L. Roediger III, and Mark A. McDaniel. 2014. *Make It Stick: The Science of Successful Learning*. Cambridge, MA: Harvard University Press.

Cuban, Larry. 2011. "Jazz, Basketball, and Teacher Decision-Making." *Larry Cuban on School Reform and Classroom Practice* (blog), June 16. https://larrycuban .wordpress.com/2011/06/16/jazz-basketball-and-teacher-decision-making.

Dyson, Anne Haas. 1993. *Social Worlds of Children Learning to Write in an Urban Primary School*. New York: Teachers College Press.

Ferguson, Ronald F., with Sarah F. Phillips, Jacob F. S. Rowley, and Jocelyn W. Friedlander. 2015. *The Influence of Teaching Beyond Standardized Test Scores: Engagement, Mindsets, and Agency*. Cambridge, MA: The Achievement Gap Initiative at Harvard University.

Fountas, Irene C., and Gay Su Pinnell. 2017. *Guided Reading: Responsive Teaching Across the Grades*. 2d edition. Portsmouth, NH: Heinemann.

Guthrie, John, and Nicole Humenick. 2004. *Motivating Students to Read: Evidence for Classroom Practices that Increase Reading Motivation and Achievement.* In P. McCardle & V. Chhabra (Eds.), "The voice of evidence in reading research" (pp. 329-354). Baltimore, MD: Paul H Brookes Publishing.

Ivey, Gay, and Peter H. Johnston. 2015. "Engaged Reading as a Collaborative Transformative Practice." *Journal of Literacy Research* 47 (3): 297–327.

Johnston, Peter H. 2004. *Choice Words: How Our Language Affects Children's Learning.* Portland, ME: Stenhouse.

Kittle, Penny. n.d. "How to Live." http://pennykittle.net/uploads/images/PDFs/Poetry/How_to_Live_imitation_by_me.pdf.

Mark, Gloria. 2008. "Work, Interrupted: The Cost of Task Switching." Interview by Kermit Pattison. *Fast Company*, July 28. www.fastcompany.com/944128/worker-interrupted-cost-task-switching.

Miller, Debbie, and Barbara Moss. 2013. *No More Independent Reading Without Support.* Portsmouth, NH: Heinemann.

National Research Council. 2000. *How People Learn: Brain, Mind, Experience, and School.* Expanded edition. Washington, DC: National Academies Press.

Newkirk, Thomas. 2016. "Seeing Anew: An Invitation to Teacher Research." *Heinemann 2016–2017 Catalog-Journal*, 6–9. Portsmouth, NH: Heinemann. www.heinemann.com/shared/onlineresources/catalogs/catalogpd16-17.pdf.

Pearson, P. David. 2011. "Toward the Next Generation of Comprehension Instruction: A Coda." In *Comprehension Going Forward: Where We Are and What's Next*, edited by Harvey Daniels, 243–254. Portsmouth, NH: Heinemann.

Ritchhart, Ron. 2002. *Intellectual Character: What It Is, Why It Matters, and How to Get It.* San Francisco: Jossey-Bass.

Sullivan, Bob, and Hugh Thompson. 2013. "Brain, Interrupted." *The New York Times Sunday Review*, May 5. www.nytimes.com/2013/05/05/opinion/sunday/a-focus-on-distraction.html.

Wiggins, Grant, and Jay McTighe. 2005. *Understanding by Design.* Expanded 2d edition. Alexandria, VA: Association for Supervision and Curriculum Development.

———. 2011. *The Understanding by Design Guide to Creating High-Quality Units.* Alexandria, VA: Association for Supervision and Curriculum Development.